A Dog's Guide to Human Hearts

Meredith Thompson

Meredith's experience

The soft glow of the early morning sun caresses the spacious kennel, casting long shadows across the polished concrete floor. The faint sound of birdsong filters through the open windows, blending with the distant barking and playful bounces of paws against the sturdy gates. It's another day in the world of dog care, a world that has become my sanctuary, my refuge from the chaotic hum of daily life. I am Meredith, and this kennel has been my haven for as long as I can remember. As I stroll along the rows of kennels, the familiar faces of the dogs greet me with eager tails wagging and bright eyes. Each one has a unique story, a personality that shines through despite the constraints of their enclosures. I pause at one particular kennel, where a gentle giant named Max rests with a dignified air, his amber eyes filled with wisdom beyond his years. Max has been at the kennel for longer than most, and his calming presence never fails to soothe my weary soul. With a small, contented smile, I greet Max and continue my rounds. The kennel is a symphony of sounds: the excited yips of puppies, the heavy panting of older dogs, and the occasional mournful howl of a newcomer adjusting to their temporary home. It's a world of constant motion, energy, and love, a world that has taught me more than any human ever could. I reach the far end of the kennel, where a spacious outdoor play area awaits the canine residents. Here, dog laughter fills the air as they frolic, chase, and wrestle with unbridled joy. The sight of them, free from the confines of their kennels, warms my heart in a way I struggle to put into words. I take a deep breath, savoring the earthy scent of freshly cut grass and the warmth of the sun on my skin. Suddenly, a playful bark pierces the serene morning, drawing my attention to the source. It's Luna, a spirited border collie known for her boundless energy and mischievous antics. She dashes around the play area, her tail a blur of excitement, and I can't help but laugh at her infectious enthusiasm. Luna's exuberance is a stark reminder of the simple joys that dogs bring into our lives, a reminder that often gets lost in the hustle and bustle of human existence. As I watch Luna weave through the agility course, a gentle breeze carries the distant scent of freshly brewed coffee from the nearby café. My stomach rumbles in response, a reminder that I haven't had breakfast yet. With a final fond glance at the dogs enjoying their playtime, I head towards the staff room, where a steaming cup of coffee and a few moments of solitude await me. The staff room is a cozy oasis, furnished with mismatched armchairs and dog-eared magazines. The familiar scent of coffee grounds lingers in the air, mingling with the comforting aroma of cinnamon and vanilla. As I brew a fresh pot of coffee, the distant murmur of voices drifts through the open window, carrying snatches of conversation and laughter from the early risers in the café. I settle into a worn armchair, cradling the warm mug of coffee in my hands. Sipping the rich, dark liquid, I let my thoughts drift back to the kennel and the dogs that have become an integral part of my life. They have taught me patience, empathy, and the true meaning of unconditional love. In their eyes, I see no judgment, no expectations—only pure, unadulterated gratitude for the simplest of gestures. As I contemplate the profound impact of dogs on our lives, the soft chime of the kennel's front door bell interrupts my reverie. Intrigued, I set down my mug and make my way to the reception area, where I find a young couple patiently waiting. The woman's eyes are bright with excitement, while the man wears a more reserved expression, a hint of uncertainty in his gaze. "Good morning," I greet them with a warm smile. "How can I help you today?" The woman steps forward, her enthusiasm bubbling over. "Hi, we're here to inquire about adopting a dog. We've been thinking about it for a while, and we finally decided that the time is right." Her words fill the air with a sense of anticipation, a hopeful energy that tugs at my heart. I recognize that look in her eyes—the same look I've seen in countless others who have found a special connection with a dog. It's a connection that transcends words, a bond forged in the quiet moments of understanding and acceptance. "I'm so glad to hear that," I reply, returning her enthusiasm. "Adopting a dog is a wonderful decision, and I'm here to help you find the perfect match. Do you have any specific traits or preferences in mind?" The couple exchanges a quick, knowing glance before the man speaks up. "We're looking for a companion who's gentle, affectionate, and good with children. We have a young daughter at home, and we want to make sure the dog will be a loving addition to our family." His words resonate with a sense of responsibility, a desire to provide a safe and loving environment for both their daughter and their future canine companion. I nod in understanding, my mind already sifting through the kennel's residents to find the ideal match. "I have a few dogs in mind who might be a great fit for your family," I assure them. "Why don't we take a walk through the kennel, and you can meet some of our residents? I'm sure we'll find the perfect match for you." As I guide the couple through the rows of kennels, their eyes light up with each enthusiastic greeting from the dogs. I introduce them to a sweet-natured terrier named Daisy, a laid-back golden retriever named Cooper, and a playful mix named Milo whose energy seems to match their own. After several introductions and thoughtful observations, the couple's attention is drawn to a quiet corner where a medium-sized dog rests with a serene expression. The dog's deep brown eyes meet theirs with a gentle warmth, and I can see the beginning of a connection blooming between them. "This is Bailey," I say, gesturing to the serene dog. "She's known for her gentle nature and her affinity for children. Would you like to spend some time with her?" The couple exchange a meaningful look, their expressions softening with a shared understanding. As they approach Bailey's kennel, the dog rises to her feet, her tail wagging in a slow, rhythmic arc. There's a palpable air of serenity surrounding her, an unspoken reassurance that seems to draw the couple closer. I step back, giving them a moment of privacy to interact with Bailey. As I observe from a respectful distance, the couple's tentative gestures gradually give way to confident strokes and soft murmurings. It's a quiet, profound exchange, unspoken words flowing between them with an understated grace. After a few moments, the couple turns to me with shimmering eyes and tender smiles. "We think Bailey might be the one," the woman says, her voice quivering with emotion. "She has this... calming presence, and we can already envision her in our home." The man nods in agreement, his expression undeniably touched. "We feel a connection with her, and we'd love to start the adoption process if she's available." My heart swells with warmth as I witness the blossoming of a new chapter in Bailey's life, a chapter that holds the promise of love, care, and belonging. "Bailey is indeed available for adoption," I confirm, my own excitement bubbling just beneath the surface. "I'll take care of the paperwork, and we'll get everything set up for her transition to your home." As the couple lingers near Bailey's kennel, their whispered conversations filled with tender promises, I leave them to their private moment and make my way back to the staff room. An unspoken sense of fulfillment pulses through me, a deep-rooted gratitude for the role I play in facilitating these poignant connections between dogs and humans. Sitting once again in the comfort of the armchair, I find myself lost in a reverie of memories and moments—each one a testament to the profound impact of dogs on our lives. From the exuberant romps of puppies to the quiet companionship of older dogs, the kennel has been witness to countless tales of love, loss, and resilience. Time slips by unnoticed, and before I know it, the sun has climbed higher in the sky, casting warm streams of light through the staff room's windows. The distant sounds of the kennel carry on the breeze, a gentle cacophony of barks, playful whines, and the occasional thud of paws against the ground. Suddenly, a familiar voice calls out from the reception area, pulling me from my thoughts. "Meredith, there's someone here to see you!" With a curious tilt of my head, I rise from the armchair and make my way to the front, where I find a man waiting with an air of quiet determination. His deep brown eyes hold a myriad of emotions—resolve, uncertainty, and a glimmer of something unspoken. "Good afternoon," I greet him with a warm smile. "How can I assist you today?" The man's gaze meets mine with a quiet intensity, a silent plea tucked within the depths of his eyes. "I'm here because... I need to find a new home for my dog." His words hang in the air, heavy with unspoken sorrow and a tinge of guilt. I can sense the weight of his decision, the ache of a heartrending choice born from circumstances beyond his control. As we lock eyes, a shared understanding passes between us, bridging the gap of unspoken emotions. "I can only imagine how difficult this must be for you," I offer gently, my tone laced with empathy. "Could you tell me a bit more about your dog? I want to ensure that we find the best possible situation for them." The man nods, his expression softening with a mix of gratitude and regret. "Her name is Sadie. She's been my companion for years, through thick and thin. But recently, my work demands have become overwhelming, and I simply can't give her the attention and care she deserves. It breaks my heart, but I know she deserves more than I can provide right now." His words carry the weight of unspoken sacrifices, the ache of a bond stretched thin by the demands of life. I offer him a sympathetic smile, a silent reassurance that he has come to the right place, a place where the needs of dogs are held in utmost regard. "I understand," I reply, my voice gentle yet unwavering. "I promise to find a loving, nurturing home for Sadie, where she'll be cherished and cared for. Would you be willing to share any specific traits or preferences that would help us find the perfect match for her?" The man nods, a glimmer of hope sparking in his eyes. "Sadie is a gentle soul, loyal and affectionate to the core. She adores long walks in the park, curling up at your feet, and being the steadfast companion you can always count on. I just want her to find a home where she'll be treasured as much as she's treasured me." His words paint a portrait of devotion, a testament to the profound bond between him and Sadie. With a silent nod, I assure him that I will do everything in my power to honor that bond, to find a home where Sadie's gentle spirit will be embraced with open arms and loving hearts. "Thank you for entrusting Sadie's future to us," I say, my voice tinged with solemn determination. "I'll do my best to find the perfect match for her. If you'd like, I can take some time to spend with Sadie and get to know her better. This way, I can understand her personality and preferences to ensure the best possible fit." At my offer, the man's shoulders visibly relax, a flicker of relief crossing his features. "I would appreciate that more than words can express," he says, his voice filled with a blend of gratitude and sorrow. "I want to make sure she finds a home where she'll be truly happy." With a comforting hand on his shoulder, I reassure him, "I'll take care of everything, and I'll keep you updated every step of the way. Sadie will be in good hands, I promise." As the man nods in silent agreement, a deep sense of purpose guides me back into the kennel, where Sadie awaits in a quiet corner, her amber eyes filled with a tangible yearning. I approach her with a gentle smile, my heart heavy with the responsibility of finding her a new beginning, a new family to call her own. For the next hour, I sit with Sadie, sharing quiet moments and soft caresses, seeking to understand the intricacies of her gentle spirit. Her presence wraps around me like a comforting embrace, a reminder of the resilience and grace that dogs embody in the face of change and uncertainty. As the afternoon draws to a close, I accompany Sadie to the outdoor play area, where the golden light of dusk bathes the world in a gentle, ethereal glow. The kennel's inhabitants have begun to wind down, their playful energy giving way to quiet contentment as the day wanes. Standing amidst the tranquil beauty of the play area, I watch as Sadie moves with a quiet grace, her movements a testament to the depth of her spirit. In the fading light, her gaze meets mine with an unspoken trust, a silent understanding that transcends the confines of words. Suddenly, the distant sound of barking draws my attention to the entrance of the play area, where an unfamiliar figure stands with tentative hesitation. It's a young woman, her eyes filled with a blend of longing and uncertainty, her hands fidgeting with nervous anticipation. "Excuse me," she calls out, her voice carrying a tinge of vulnerability. "I'm here to inquire about adopting a dog... if that's possible." The raw emotion in her voice tugs at my heart, igniting a spark of hope within me. I gesture for her to approach, my eyes meeting hers with a gentle warmth. "Of course, I'd be happy to help you find the perfect companion. Do you have any specific traits or preferences in mind?" As she draws closer, her gaze falls upon Sadie, and a soft gasp escapes her lips. "She's... she's beautiful. Can I spend some time with her?" Moved by the emotion in her voice, I offer her a reassuring smile. "Absolutely. Sadie would be delighted to meet you. Take all the time you need to get to know her, and I'll be here when you're ready to talk." With a tentative nod, the young woman enters the play area, her steps hesitant yet filled with a palpable longing. I linger by the entrance, giving them the space to form their own connection, to find the unspoken bond that can only be forged through shared moments and understanding. As I watch from a respectful distance, the young woman's gestures gradually grow more confident, her tentative touches giving way to gentle strokes and murmured reassurances. Sadie, in turn, responds with a quiet grace, welcoming the young woman's presence with an unassuming warmth. Time seems to stretch and fold within the tranquil confines of the play area, each passing moment holding the promise of a new beginning—a beginning born from the unsung depths of empathy, compassion, and shared understanding. After a while, the young woman turns to me, her eyes shimmering with unshed tears and a radiant hope. "I think Sadie might be the one," she says, her voice barely above a whisper. "There's this... unspoken connection between us, a flicker of understanding that I can't quite put into words." Her words echo the sentiments of countless others who have found their hearts intertwined with those of the dogs they've chosen to welcome into their lives. I find myself nodding in quiet agreement, my heart swelling with the profound sense of fulfillment that comes from catalyzing such poignant connections. "I'm so glad to hear that," I reply, my voice suffused with genuine warmth. "I'll take care of the paperwork and ensure that everything is set for Sadie's transition to your home. She'll be a cherished addition to your family, I'm sure of it." As the young woman lingers in the play area, her whispered conversations with Sadie filled with tender promises and hopeful reassurances, I leave them to their private moment and make my way back to the staff room. A quiet sense of satisfaction courses through me, a profound gratitude for the opportunity to facilitate these poignant intersections of lives and hearts. Seated once more in the familiar embrace of the armchair, I find myself enveloped in a hushed tranquility, my thoughts drifting back to the countless dogs whose paths have intertwined with mine. Each one has left an indelible mark on my heart, teaching me invaluable lessons in love, resilience, and the unspoken language of gratitude. The fading light of dusk filters through the staff room's windows, casting warm, golden hues across the worn wooden floor. In the distance, the kennel's inhabitants have settled into a peaceful calm, their gentle murmurs and contented sighs weaving a tranquil tapestry of sound. Suddenly, the familiar sound of paws trotting down the hallway draws my attention, and I glance up to find a sight that fills my heart with unexpected joy. It's Max, the gentle giant whose quiet wisdom has always held a special place in my heart, making his way towards me with a deliberate purpose. With a deep rumble of approval, Max halts in front of my armchair, his amber eyes reflecting a quiet understanding that transcends the confines of human speech. His presence alone is a balm to my weary soul, a silent reassurance that no words could adequately convey. "Hey there, old friend," I murmur, reaching out to offer him a reassuring pat. Max leans into my touch, his tail wagging in slow, deliberate arcs, as though affirming the unspoken bond between us. In the soft glow of dusk, a sense of gratitude washes over me, a profound appreciation for the unwavering companionship of dogs and the countless lessons they impart through their unassuming presence. As if sensing the weight of my thoughts, Max emits a deep, rumbling hum, a sound that resonates with a quiet reassurance and a timeless wisdom that has always put my heart at ease. It's a sound that speaks volumes, carrying the essence of gratitude in its gentle cadence. The sense of gratitude pushed me to write the pages of this book to convey to as many people the meaning of having a dog in one's life. I wanted to imagine what dogs thought about their human friends and what lessons they tried to convey to them.

Happy reading and happy life to everyone

Meredith Thompson

Finding Purpose

1.1 Discovering the Joy of Companionship

Dogs are known for their unwavering loyalty and unconditional love. They have an innate ability to form deep connections with humans, bringing joy and companionship into their lives. In this chapter, we will explore the profound impact that dogs have on the human heart and the joy they bring to our lives.

1.1.1 The Power of a Dog's Presence

There is something truly special about the presence of a dog. Their mere existence can bring comfort and solace to those around them. Dogs have an incredible ability to sense our emotions and provide us with the support we need, even without uttering a single word. They have an uncanny knack for knowing when we are sad, and they will do everything in their power to lift our spirits.

When we come home after a long and tiring day, our faithful canine companions are always there to greet us with wagging tails and wet kisses. Their enthusiasm and excitement are contagious, instantly brightening our mood and reminding us of the simple joys in life. Dogs have an innate ability to live in the present moment, and they teach us to do the same. They remind us to appreciate the little things and find happiness in the everyday moments.

1.1.2 Finding Meaning in Everyday Moments

Dogs have a unique way of finding meaning in the simplest of moments. Whether it's chasing a ball in the park, going for a leisurely walk, or curling up beside us on the couch, they find joy in the ordinary. They teach us to slow down and appreciate the beauty that surrounds us. Through their eyes, we learn to find happiness in the small gestures of love and the quiet moments of companionship.

A dog's love is pure and unconditional. They don't care about our flaws or imperfections; they love us for who we are. They teach us the true meaning of acceptance and remind us that we are worthy of love, just as we are. Dogs have an incredible ability to heal our hearts and mend our souls. They provide us with a sense of purpose and remind us of the power of love.

1.1.3 Teaching Humans to Love Unconditionally

One of the greatest lessons dogs teach us is the art of loving unconditionally. They don't hold grudges or keep score; they love us wholeheartedly, no matter what. Dogs have an incredible capacity for forgiveness and teach us to let go of anger and resentment. They show us that love is not about keeping tabs or expecting something in return; it is about giving without expecting anything in return.

Through their unwavering love, dogs teach us to be more compassionate and understanding towards others. They show us that love knows no boundaries and that it is possible to find common ground even in the most challenging of circumstances. Dogs have an incredible ability to bridge gaps and bring people together. They remind us that love has the power to heal and unite.

1.1.4 Discovering the Joy of Companionship

In the journey of life, dogs are our constant companions. They stand by our side through thick and thin, offering us unwavering support and love. They teach us the true meaning of loyalty and remind us of the importance of being there for one another. Dogs have an incredible ability to bring out the best in us and inspire us to be better human beings.

1.2 Teaching Humans to Love Unconditionally

Dogs have an innate ability to love unconditionally. They don't judge, hold grudges, or place conditions on their affection. They simply love with all their hearts, no matter what. In this chapter, we will explore how dogs teach humans to love unconditionally and the profound impact it can have on our lives.

1.2.1 The Power of Acceptance

One of the most beautiful lessons dogs teach us is the power of acceptance. They accept us for who we are, flaws and all. They don't care about our appearance, our status, or our past mistakes. Dogs see beyond all of that and love us purely for being ourselves. They teach us to embrace our imperfections and to love ourselves unconditionally.

1.2.2 Embracing Vulnerability

Dogs have an incredible ability to sense our emotions and provide comfort when we need it most. They create a safe space for us to be vulnerable and express our true feelings without fear of judgment. Through their unwavering support and affection, dogs teach us to open our hearts and trust in the power of vulnerability. They show us that it is okay to let our guard down and allow ourselves to be loved.

1.2.3 Forgiving and Letting Go

Humans often hold onto grudges and find it difficult to forgive. Dogs, on the other hand, have a remarkable capacity for forgiveness. No matter how many times we may accidentally step on their paws or forget to fill their food bowl, dogs forgive us instantly. They teach us the importance of letting go of anger and resentment, and instead, focus on the love and joy that surrounds us.

1.2.4 Unconditional Love in Action

Dogs demonstrate their unconditional love through their actions. They are always there for us, ready to offer a comforting paw or a wagging tail. They listen without judgment, provide companionship during our loneliest moments, and celebrate our victories with unbridled enthusiasm. Dogs teach us that love is not just a feeling but a verb, something to be expressed through our actions and choices.

1.2.5 Teaching Empathy and Compassion

Dogs have an incredible ability to sense when we are sad, anxious, or in need of comfort. They offer a listening ear, a warm snuggle, or a gentle nudge to remind us that we are not alone. Through their presence, dogs teach us empathy and compassion. They show us the importance of being there for others, of offering a shoulder to lean on, and of providing comfort in times of need.

1.2.6 The Healing Power of Love

Love has a profound healing effect on both humans and dogs. Dogs have been known to provide emotional support and therapy to individuals facing physical or mental health challenges. Their unconditional love and unwavering loyalty can bring solace and comfort during difficult times. Dogs teach us that love has the power to heal wounds, mend broken hearts, and bring joy back into our lives.

1.2.7 Embracing the Present Moment

Dogs live in the present moment, fully immersed in the here and now. They don't dwell on the past or worry about the future. Dogs teach us to embrace the present moment and find joy in the simple pleasures of life. They remind us to stop and smell the flowers, to savor each bite of food, and to appreciate the beauty that surrounds us. Through their example, dogs teach us to live more mindfully and to find happiness in the present.

By embodying unconditional love themselves, dogs have the power to inspire humans to love unconditionally as well. When we witness the pure and unwavering love of a dog, it touches something deep within us. It reminds us of the capacity we have to love without limits and to extend that love to others. Dogs teach us that by loving unconditionally, we can create a ripple effect of love and kindness that can transform the world.

1.3 Finding Meaning in Everyday Moments

Every day is filled with countless moments that may seem insignificant at first glance. But for a dog, these everyday moments hold a special significance. Dogs have an innate ability to find meaning in the simplest of things, and they teach us humans to do the same. In this chapter, we will explore how dogs help us find meaning in our everyday lives and how we can learn to appreciate the beauty in the ordinary.

1.3.1 Embracing the Present Moment

Dogs have an incredible talent for living in the present moment. They don't dwell on the past or worry about the future. Instead, they fully immerse themselves in the here and now. Whether it's chasing a ball, enjoying a belly rub, or simply basking in the warmth of the sun, dogs remind us to embrace the present moment and find joy in the little things.

When we take a moment to observe our furry friends, we realize that they find happiness in the simplest of activities. They teach us that life is not about the grand gestures or the extraordinary events, but about finding contentment in the everyday moments. Whether it's the wag of a tail, the sound of a familiar voice, or the touch of a gentle hand, dogs show us that true happiness can be found in the ordinary.

1.3.2 Appreciating the Beauty of Nature

Dogs have an innate connection with nature. They revel in the sights, sounds, and smells of the great outdoors. Whether it's a leisurely walk in the park or a romp in the fields, dogs remind us to appreciate the beauty that surrounds us. They teach us to pause and take in the vibrant colors of a sunset, the soothing sound of rustling leaves, and the invigorating scent of fresh grass.

In our busy lives, we often forget to stop and admire the wonders of nature. But dogs, with their keen senses and boundless curiosity, remind us to slow down and appreciate the world around us. They show us that even in the midst of chaos, there is beauty to be found if we take the time to look.

1.3.3 Finding Joy in Simple Pleasures

Dogs have an uncanny ability to find joy in the simplest of pleasures. Whether it's a game of fetch, a delicious treat, or a cozy nap, dogs remind us that happiness can be found in the most ordinary moments. They teach us to let go of our worries and embrace the simple joys that life has to offer.

When we watch a dog chase its tail or roll around in the grass with pure delight, we can't help but smile. Dogs show us that it's not the material possessions or the extravagant experiences that bring us true happiness, but the simple pleasures that are within our reach every day. They remind us to find joy in the laughter of a loved one, the taste of a home-cooked meal, or the warmth of a cozy blanket.

1.3.4 Cultivating Gratitude and Mindfulness

Dogs are masters of gratitude and mindfulness. They appreciate every act of kindness, no matter how small, and they never take anything for granted. Whether it's a pat on the head, a scratch behind the ears, or a loving gaze, dogs show us the power of gratitude and the importance of being present in the moment.

By observing our canine companions, we can learn to cultivate gratitude and mindfulness in our own lives. We can learn to appreciate the love and support of our friends and family, the beauty of nature, and the simple pleasures that bring us joy. Dogs teach us that by being fully present and grateful for what we have, we can find meaning and fulfillment in our everyday lives.

1.3.5 Creating Lasting Memories

Dogs have a way of creating lasting memories in our lives. Whether it's the first time they greet us with a wagging tail, the adventures we embark on together, or the quiet moments of companionship, dogs leave an indelible mark on our hearts. They remind us to cherish the memories we create and to hold onto them long after our furry friends are gone.

In the hustle and bustle of life, it's easy to forget the importance of creating memories. But dogs, with their unwavering loyalty and unconditional love, show us that memories are the threads that weave the tapestry of our lives. They teach us to savor the moments we share with our loved ones, to capture the beauty of everyday life, and to create memories that will bring us comfort and joy in the years to come.

In conclusion, dogs have a remarkable ability to find meaning in everyday moments. They teach us to embrace the present moment, appreciate the beauty of nature, find joy in simple pleasures, cultivate gratitude and mindfulness, and create lasting memories. By following their lead, we can learn to find meaning and fulfillment in our own lives, and truly appreciate the beauty that surrounds us. So let us take a moment to pause, observe, and learn from our furry friends, for they have much wisdom to share.

1.4 The Power of a Dog's Presence

Dogs have an incredible ability to make a profound impact on the lives of humans. Their presence alone can bring comfort, joy, and a sense of purpose. In this chapter, we will explore the power of a dog's presence and how it can transform the lives of those around them.

1.4.1 A Constant Companion

One of the most remarkable aspects of a dog's presence is their unwavering loyalty and companionship. Dogs have an innate ability to sense when their humans are in need of comfort or support. Whether it's a gentle nudge, a wagging tail, or simply sitting quietly by their side, dogs have an intuitive understanding of how to provide solace during difficult times. Their presence alone can be a source of strength and reassurance, reminding us that we are never alone.

1.4.2 A Source of Unconditional Love

Dogs are masters of unconditional love. They don't judge, hold grudges, or place conditions on their affection. Their love is pure and unwavering, regardless of our flaws or mistakes. This unconditional love can have a profound impact on our emotional well-being. It reminds us that we are worthy of love and acceptance, just as we are. A dog's presence can help heal emotional wounds, boost self-esteem, and provide a sense of belonging.

1.4.3 A Catalyst for Connection

Dogs have a unique ability to bring people together. Whether it's through a shared love for dogs or simply the joy they bring to a room, dogs have a way of breaking down barriers and fostering connections. Their presence can create a sense of community and belonging, allowing people to bond over their shared experiences and love for these incredible creatures. Dogs have a way of bringing out the best in us and reminding us of the importance of human connection.

1.4.4 A Source of Comfort and Emotional Support

The power of a dog's presence extends beyond mere companionship. Dogs have been known to provide emotional support to those in need, whether it's individuals struggling with mental health issues, survivors of trauma, or those facing challenging life circumstances. Their intuitive nature allows them to sense when we are feeling down or anxious, and they respond with a comforting presence that can help alleviate stress and provide a sense of calm. Dogs have a unique ability to understand our emotions and offer solace without judgment or expectation.

1.4.5 A Teacher of Mindfulness

Dogs are masters of living in the present moment. They don't dwell on the past or worry about the future. Instead, they fully embrace the here and now, finding joy in the simplest of pleasures. Their presence serves as a reminder for us to slow down, appreciate the beauty around us, and find happiness in the present moment. Dogs teach us the importance of mindfulness and living a life filled with gratitude and joy.

1.4.6 A Mirror to Our Hearts

A dog's presence can also serve as a mirror to our own hearts. They have an uncanny ability to reflect our emotions and behaviors back to us, allowing us to see ourselves more clearly. Dogs can sense when we are happy, sad, or in need of comfort, and they respond accordingly. Their presence can help us become more self-aware, encouraging us to examine our own actions and emotions. Through their unconditional love and unwavering loyalty, dogs inspire us to become better versions of ourselves.

In conclusion, the power of a dog's presence is truly remarkable. Their unwavering loyalty, unconditional love, and ability to bring people together make them invaluable companions. Dogs have a unique way of providing comfort, emotional support, and teaching us important life lessons. Their presence reminds us of the beauty of living in the present moment and the importance of human connection. Dogs have a profound impact on our lives, and their presence is a gift that should be cherished and celebrated.

Lessons in Laughter

2.1 Bringing Smiles and Laughter to Human Lives

Dogs have an incredible ability to bring joy and laughter into the lives of humans. Their playful nature, unconditional love, and infectious enthusiasm can brighten even the darkest of days. In this chapter, we will explore the ways in which dogs bring smiles and laughter to human lives, and the profound impact they have on our well-being.

2.1.1 The Power of a Wagging Tail

One of the simplest yet most effective ways dogs bring smiles to our faces is through their wagging tails. There is something undeniably heartwarming about coming home to a dog who is overjoyed to see you. Their wagging tail is a clear expression of their happiness and love, and it is impossible not to be affected by their enthusiasm. Whether we've had a long day at work or are feeling down, the sight of a wagging tail can instantly lift our spirits and bring a smile to our faces.

2.1.2 Silly Antics and Playful Moments

Dogs have an innate ability to find joy in the simplest of things. Whether it's chasing their own tail, playing with a squeaky toy, or rolling around in the grass, their silly antics never fail to bring laughter to our lives. Their playful nature is infectious, and it reminds us to embrace our inner child and find joy in the little things. Dogs teach us the importance of not taking life too seriously and finding happiness in the present moment.

2.1.3 The Healing Power of Laughter

Laughter is often referred to as the best medicine, and dogs have a unique talent for eliciting laughter from their human companions. Numerous studies have shown that laughter has a positive impact on our physical and mental well-being. It reduces stress, boosts our immune system, and improves our overall mood. Dogs, with their playful antics and humorous expressions, have an uncanny ability to make us laugh even when we're feeling down. They remind us to find humor in life's challenges and to approach difficult situations with a lighthearted perspective.

2.1.4 Unconditional Love and Acceptance

One of the reasons dogs bring so much joy and laughter into our lives is their unwavering love and acceptance. They don't judge us for our flaws or imperfections; instead, they love us unconditionally, flaws and all. This unconditional love creates a safe and nurturing environment where we can be ourselves without fear of judgment. Dogs teach us the importance of accepting and loving ourselves, which in turn allows us to find joy and laughter in our own lives.

2.1.5 The Power of Connection

Dogs have an incredible ability to connect with humans on a deep emotional level. They can sense our moods, provide comfort when we're feeling down, and celebrate with us during moments of joy. Their ability to empathize and understand our emotions is truly remarkable. Through their companionship, dogs teach us the importance of human connection and remind us that we are never alone in this world. Their presence brings a sense of belonging and fills our lives with laughter and love.

2.1.6 Spreading Happiness to Others

Not only do dogs bring joy and laughter to their immediate human companions, but they also have a ripple effect on those around them. Whether it's a friendly encounter on a walk, a visit to a nursing home, or participating in therapy programs, dogs have the power to bring smiles to the faces of strangers. Their presence alone can brighten someone's day and provide a momentary escape from their troubles. Dogs teach us the importance of spreading happiness and kindness to others, and the profound impact it can have on their lives.

In conclusion, dogs have a remarkable ability to bring smiles and laughter to human lives. Through their wagging tails, silly antics, and unconditional love, they remind us to find joy in the present moment and to embrace the simple pleasures of life. Their healing power of laughter and their ability to connect with us on a deep emotional level is truly extraordinary. Dogs teach us the importance of spreading happiness and kindness to others, and they leave an indelible mark on our hearts. So, let us cherish the laughter and joy that dogs bring into our lives and be grateful for the unbreakable bond we share with our furry friends.

2.2 The Healing Power of Humor

Humor has a unique ability to heal and bring joy to our lives. As dogs, we have an innate understanding of this power and use it to brighten the days of our human companions. In this chapter, we will explore the healing power of humor and how it can create moments of joy and laughter in the lives of humans.

2.2.1 The Importance of Laughter

Laughter is a universal language that transcends barriers and brings people together. It has the remarkable ability to lift spirits, ease tension, and create a sense of connection. As dogs, we have a natural talent for bringing smiles to the faces of our human friends. Whether it's through our silly antics, playful behavior, or the way we look at the world with innocent eyes, we have the power to make even the toughest days a little brighter.

2.2.2 The Healing Effects of Laughter

Laughter has been scientifically proven to have numerous health benefits. It releases endorphins, the body's natural feel-good chemicals, which can reduce stress, boost the immune system, and improve overall well-being. When humans laugh, their bodies relax, and their minds become more open to positive experiences. As dogs, we instinctively know how to tap into this healing power of laughter and bring it into the lives of our human companions.

2.2.3 Creating Moments of Joy

One of our greatest gifts as dogs is our ability to create moments of joy in the lives of humans. Whether it's through our playful antics, our unconditional love, or our ability to find joy in the simplest of things, we have a knack for bringing smiles to the faces of those around us. We remind humans to take a break from their worries and enjoy the present moment. By engaging in play and laughter, we help them let go of their troubles and find happiness in the here and now.

2.2.4 The Power of Humor in Difficult Times

Humor can be a powerful tool in helping humans navigate through difficult times. It provides a temporary escape from the challenges they face and offers a fresh perspective on their problems. As dogs, we have an uncanny ability to sense when our human friends are feeling down or stressed. We use our playful nature and sense of humor to lift their spirits and remind them that there is always a reason to smile, even in the darkest of times.

2.2.5 The Bond Strengthened Through Laughter

When humans and dogs share moments of laughter, a special bond is formed. Laughter creates a sense of connection and deepens the relationship between humans and their furry companions. It fosters a sense of trust, understanding, and mutual joy.

Through laughter, we communicate on a level that goes beyond words, forging an unbreakable bond that brings immense happiness to both parties.

2.2.6 Spreading Laughter and Joy

As dogs, we have a responsibility to spread laughter and joy wherever we go. Our playful nature and ability to find humor in the simplest of things can have a profound impact on the lives of those around us. By bringing smiles to the faces of strangers, we create a ripple effect of positivity and happiness. We remind humans to embrace their inner child, to find joy in the little things, and to never underestimate the power of laughter.

In conclusion, the healing power of humor is a remarkable gift that dogs bring into the lives of humans. Through our playful nature, silly antics, and ability to find joy in the simplest of things, we could lift spirits, ease tension, and create moments of laughter and joy. By embracing the healing power of humor, humans can find solace, strength, and a renewed sense of happiness. So let us continue to spread laughter and joy, for in doing so, we not only brighten the lives of our human companions but also enrich our own lives in immeasurable ways.

2.3 Creating Moments of Joy

As dogs, one of our greatest gifts to humans is the ability to create moments of joy. We have an innate ability to bring happiness and laughter into the lives of those around us. In this chapter, we will explore the various ways in which we can create these moments of joy and the profound impact they have on human hearts.

2.3.1 Spreading Smiles and Laughter

One of the simplest yet most powerful ways we create moments of joy is through our ability to bring smiles and laughter to human lives. Our playful nature and silly antics never fail to brighten the mood and uplift spirits. Whether it's chasing our tails, playing fetch, or simply goofing around, our playful energy is contagious and brings a sense of lightness to any situation.

2.3.2 The Healing Power of Laughter

Laughter has a remarkable ability to heal and bring people together. It is a universal language that transcends barriers and connects us on a deep level. As dogs, we understand this power and use it to heal the hearts of humans. Our ability to make people laugh not only brings them joy in the present moment but also helps them cope with difficult times. Laughter has a way of easing pain, reducing stress, and reminding humans of the beauty and humor in life.

2.3.3 Finding Joy in Everyday Moments

Humans often get caught up in the busyness of life and forget to appreciate the simple joys that surround them. As dogs, we have a unique perspective that allows us to find joy in the smallest of things. Whether it's chasing butterflies, rolling in the grass, or simply enjoying a belly rub, we remind humans to slow down and savor the present moment. By sharing in these everyday joys, we help humans rediscover the beauty and wonder of the world around them.

2.3.4 The Importance of Playfulness

Playfulness is not just a source of entertainment; it is also a vital component of a fulfilling life. Through play, humans can tap into their creativity, reduce stress, and strengthen relationships. As dogs, we are experts in the art of playfulness. We encourage humans to let go of their inhibitions, embrace their inner child, and engage in activities that bring them joy. Whether it's a game of fetch, a romp in the park, or a playful wrestle, these moments of playfulness create lasting memories and deepen the bond between humans and dogs.

2.3.5 Creating Lasting Memories

Moments of joy are not fleeting; they leave a lasting imprint on the hearts and minds of humans. As dogs, we have the ability to create memories that humans cherish for a lifetime. Whether it's the first time a child experiences the unconditional love of a dog, the laughter shared during a family game night, or the joy of a long walk on a sunny day, these memories become treasured moments that humans hold dear. By creating these moments of joy, we leave an indelible mark on the lives of those we love.

2.3.6 The Power of Connection

Creating moments of joy is not just about bringing happiness to individuals; it is also about fostering a sense of connection and belonging. When humans experience joy together, it strengthens their bond and deepens their relationships. As dogs, we have the ability to bring people together, to bridge gaps, and to create a sense of unity. Whether it's through a shared love for a dog or a shared moment of laughter, we remind humans of their common humanity and the importance of connection.

In conclusion, creating moments of joy is a fundamental part of our purpose as dogs. Through our playful nature, our ability to bring smiles and laughter, and our knack for finding joy in everyday moments, we have the power to touch human hearts in profound ways. These moments of joy not only bring happiness and laughter but also strengthen relationships, foster connection, and leave lasting memories. By embracing our role as bringers of joy, we can make a positive impact on the lives of those around us and remind humans of the beauty and wonder of life.

2.4 The Importance of Playfulness

Playfulness is an essential aspect of a dog's life. It is not just a form of entertainment or a way to pass the time; it is a fundamental part of who we are as dogs. Playfulness allows us to express our joy, curiosity, and enthusiasm for life. It is through play that we learn, grow, and form deeper connections with our human companions.

2.4.1 The Joy of Play

Play brings immense joy to both dogs and humans. When we engage in play, whether it's chasing a ball, playing tug-of-war, or simply frolicking in the grass, we experience a sense of pure happiness. Our tails wag with excitement, our eyes sparkle with delight, and our hearts fill with joy. In those moments, all worries and troubles fade away, and we are fully present in the joy of the present moment.

2.4.2 Strengthening the Bond

Playfulness is not just about having fun; it also strengthens the bond between dogs and humans. When we play together, we create shared experiences and memories that deepen our connection. Through play, we learn to trust and rely on each other. We develop a mutual understanding and a language of play that transcends words. It is in these moments of playfulness that the bond between us grows stronger and more resilient.

2.4.3 Promoting Physical and Mental Well-being

Playfulness is not only beneficial for our emotional well-being but also for our physical and mental health. When we engage in physical activities such as running, jumping, and playing fetch, we exercise our bodies, keeping them strong and healthy. Play also stimulates our minds, keeping us mentally sharp and alert. It helps us learn new skills, problem-solve, and adapt to different situations.

2.4.4 Teaching Humans to Embrace Playfulness

As dogs, we have a natural ability to bring out the playful side in humans. Our infectious enthusiasm and boundless energy can inspire even the most serious and reserved individuals to let go and embrace their inner child. Through play, we teach humans to let loose, to laugh, and to find joy in the simplest of things. We show them that life is meant to be enjoyed and that playfulness is an essential part of a fulfilling life.

2.4.5 Creating Moments of Connection

Playfulness creates moments of connection and shared joy between dogs and humans. When we engage in play together, we are fully present in the moment, focused on each other and the activity at hand. These moments of connection go beyond words and deepen the bond between us. Through play, we communicate our love, affection, and appreciation for one another. It is in these moments that we truly understand the power of playfulness in fostering love and connection.

2.4.6 Embracing Playfulness in Everyday Life

Playfulness is not limited to specific activities or designated playtimes. It is a mindset, a way of approaching life with a sense of curiosity, wonder, and joy. As dogs, we find playfulness in the simplest of things – a fallen leaf, a squeaky toy, or a game of hide-and-seek. We invite humans to embrace playfulness in their everyday lives, to find joy in the mundane, and to approach challenges with a playful spirit. By doing so, they can experience life in a more vibrant and fulfilling way.

2.4.7 The Healing Power of Play

Playfulness has a remarkable healing power. It can lift spirits, alleviate stress, and bring comfort in times of sadness or difficulty. When humans engage in play with us, their worries and troubles momentarily fade away, replaced by laughter and joy. Playfulness has the ability to heal emotional wounds, mend broken hearts, and bring light to even the darkest of days. It reminds us that no matter what challenges we face, there is always room for play and laughter.

In conclusion, playfulness is not just a frivolous activity; it is an essential part of a dog's life and a powerful tool for fostering love, connection, and joy. Through play, we teach humans to embrace their inner child, to find joy in the simplest of things, and to approach life with a playful spirit. So, let us all embrace playfulness and experience the profound joy and connection it brings to our lives.

Unbreakable Bonds

3.1 Forging Lifelong Connections

Dogs are known for their ability to form deep and lasting connections with humans. From the moment we enter their lives, they shower us with unconditional love and loyalty. They become our companions, our confidants, and our best friends. In this chapter, we explore the profound bond that is forged between dogs and humans, a bond that transcends time and leaves an indelible mark on our hearts.

3.1.1 The Power of Trust

Trust is the foundation of any strong relationship, and the bond between a dog and a human is no exception. Dogs have an innate ability to trust us completely, even when we may not trust ourselves. They rely on us for their basic needs, but more than that, they trust us with their emotions and vulnerabilities. They teach us the importance of being trustworthy and dependable, and in return, they offer us their unwavering loyalty.

Life is full of ups and downs, and during our darkest moments, dogs are there to provide comfort and support. They have an uncanny ability to sense when we are feeling sad or distressed, and they offer us their presence and affection without judgment. They remind us that we are never alone, and their unwavering support helps us navigate through life's challenges with strength and resilience.

3.1.3 The Heartache of Saying Goodbye

One of the most difficult aspects of the bond between a dog and a human is the inevitable goodbye. Dogs have shorter lifespans than humans, and saying farewell to our beloved companions is a heart-wrenching experience. However, the love and memories we share with them remain etched in our hearts forever. They teach us the importance of cherishing every moment and valuing the time we have with our loved ones.

3.1.4 The Legacy of Love

Although dogs may physically leave our lives, their love and impact continue to shape us long after they are gone. Their legacy lives on in the lessons they taught us, the joy they brought us, and the love they shared with us. Their presence may no longer be tangible, but their spirit remains alive in our hearts. We carry their love with us, and it influences the way we interact with others and the world around us.

When we lose a beloved dog, it is natural to grieve and mourn their loss. However, we can also find solace in honoring their memory. Whether it is through creating a memorial, sharing stories and photos, or supporting animal welfare causes, we can keep their spirit alive and continue to spread the love they brought into our lives. By honoring their memory, we ensure that their impact on us and the world is never forgotten.

3.1.6 The Lifelong Connection

The bond between a dog and a human is a lifelong connection that transcends time and space. It is a relationship built on trust, love, and mutual understanding. Dogs teach us valuable lessons about loyalty, forgiveness, and the power of unconditional love. They remind us to live in the present moment and find joy in the simplest of pleasures. Through their unwavering companionship, they show us the true meaning of friendship and the depth of our capacity to love.

In the next chapter, we delve into the lessons dogs teach us about self-love and the power of unconditional love. We explore how they help us overcome fear and open our hearts to the possibilities of love and connection. Join us as we uncover the transformative power of a dog's love in Chapter 4: "Lessons in Love."

3.2 The Trust Between Dog and Human

Dogs are known for their unwavering loyalty and unconditional love towards their human companions. This deep bond between a dog and a human is built on a foundation of trust. In this chapter, we will explore the trust that exists between dogs and humans, and how it forms the basis for a strong and meaningful relationship.

3.2.1 Trusting Instincts

Dogs have an incredible ability to sense and understand human emotions. They can pick up on subtle cues and body language, allowing them to gauge the emotional state of their human companions. This heightened sense of perception enables dogs to provide comfort and support when their humans are feeling down or stressed.

When a dog senses fear or anxiety in their human, they instinctively respond with reassurance and comfort. They offer a calming presence and provide a sense of security, allowing their humans to trust in their ability to protect and care for them. This mutual trust creates a bond that goes beyond words and is built on a deep understanding of each other's needs.

3.2.2 Dependability and Reliability

Dogs are known for their unwavering loyalty and dependability. They are always there for their humans, ready to offer a listening ear or a comforting paw. This reliability builds trust between a dog and their human, as they know they can always count on their furry friend to be by their side through thick and thin.

A dog's consistent presence and unwavering support create a sense of security and trust in their human companion. They become a constant source of comfort and stability, providing a safe space where their human can be themselves without fear of judgment or rejection. This trust allows for open and honest communication, strengthening the bond between dog and human.

3.2.3 Mutual Understanding

Dogs have an innate ability to understand their humans on a deep level. They can sense their moods, anticipate their needs, and provide comfort without the need for words. This mutual understanding fosters trust between a dog and their human, as they know that their furry companion truly understands and accepts them for who they are.

Through their actions and behaviors, dogs show their humans that they are loved and cherished unconditionally. This acceptance creates a safe and trusting environment where humans can be vulnerable and authentic. Dogs teach us the importance of embracing our true selves and finding solace in the love and acceptance of others.

3.2.4 Building Trust Through Training

Training plays a crucial role in building trust between a dog and their human. Through positive reinforcement and consistent guidance, dogs learn to trust their humans as reliable leaders. This trust allows dogs to feel secure in their human's decisions and guidance, knowing that their best interests are always at heart.

As humans invest time and effort into training their dogs, they demonstrate their commitment to their furry companion's well-being. This commitment builds trust and strengthens the bond between dog and human. Dogs learn to trust that their humans will provide them with the necessary guidance and care, while humans trust that their dogs will follow their lead and behave appropriately.

3.2.5 Trusting Each Other's Intentions

Trust between a dog and their human is not one-sided. Humans also need to trust their dogs and believe in their intentions. Dogs are inherently good-natured and have a genuine desire to please their humans. By trusting in their dog's intentions, humans allow their furry friends to flourish and showcase their loyalty and love.

Trusting a dog's instincts and judgment is an essential aspect of the bond between dog and human. Dogs have an uncanny ability to sense danger and protect their humans from harm. By trusting in their dog's instincts, humans can feel safe and secure, knowing that their loyal companion will always have their back.

In conclusion, the trust between a dog and a human is a powerful and unbreakable bond. It is built on instincts, dependability, mutual understanding, training, and trusting each other's intentions. Dogs teach us the importance of trust in relationships and remind us of the incredible love and loyalty that can exist between two beings. Through trust, dogs and humans create a deep and meaningful connection that enriches both their lives.

3.3 Supporting Each Other Through Difficult Times

Dogs have an incredible ability to sense when their humans are going through difficult times. Whether it's a physical ailment, emotional distress, or a challenging life situation, dogs have an innate sense of empathy and a natural inclination to provide comfort and support. In this chapter, we will explore the ways in which dogs support their humans through difficult times and the profound impact they have on their well-being.

3.3.1 A Shoulder to Lean On

When humans face adversity, they often find solace in the presence of their furry companions. Dogs have an uncanny ability to sense when their humans are feeling down or distressed. They will instinctively come close, offering a comforting presence and a shoulder to lean on. Their unconditional love and non-judgmental nature create a safe space for humans to express their emotions without fear of being judged or misunderstood.

3.3.2 Easing Emotional Pain

Dogs have a remarkable ability to ease emotional pain. They can sense when their humans are feeling sad, anxious, or stressed, and they respond with gentle affection and unwavering loyalty. Their presence alone can provide a sense of calm and reassurance, helping to alleviate feelings of loneliness and despair. Dogs have a unique way of bringing joy and laughter into our lives, even during the darkest of times.

3.3.3 A Listening Ear

One of the most valuable ways in which dogs support their humans is by being excellent listeners. They may not understand the words we say, but they can sense the emotions behind them. Dogs will patiently sit by our side, attentively listening to our stories, fears, and worries. They offer a non-judgmental ear, allowing us to unload our burdens and find comfort in their silent understanding. Sometimes, all we need is someone to listen, and dogs excel at fulfilling that role.

3.3.4 Unconditional Love and Acceptance

During difficult times, humans often struggle with feelings of self-doubt and worthlessness. Dogs, however, see us through a lens of unconditional love and acceptance. They don't care about our flaws, mistakes, or imperfections. Dogs love us for who we are, without any conditions or expectations. Their unwavering devotion reminds us that we are worthy of love and that we are deserving of compassion, even when we find it hard to believe in ourselves.

3.3.5 Providing a Sense of Purpose

When humans face challenging circumstances, they may lose sight of their purpose or feel overwhelmed by the weight of their struggles. Dogs have a unique way of reminding us of our purpose and giving us a reason to keep going. They rely on us for their well-being, and in return, they inspire us to be the best version of ourselves. Dogs teach us the importance of resilience, determination, and finding joy in the simplest of moments.

3.3.6 Healing Through Physical Touch

Physical touch has a profound impact on our well-being, especially during difficult times. Dogs instinctively know this and offer their humans the healing power of touch. A gentle pat on the head, a warm snuggle, or a comforting paw on our lap can provide immense comfort and reassurance. The physical presence of a dog can help reduce stress, lower blood pressure, and release feel-good hormones, promoting overall emotional and physical well-being.

3.3.7 A Source of Strength and Inspiration

Dogs have an incredible ability to inspire their humans to persevere through difficult times. Their unwavering loyalty, resilience, and ability to find joy in the simplest of moments serve as a reminder that there is always hope, even in the darkest of times. Dogs teach us to live in the present moment, to appreciate the small joys in life, and to find strength in the face of adversity. Their presence alone can ignite a spark of determination and resilience within us.

3.3.8 The Healing Power of Play

During challenging times, dogs can be a source of much-needed laughter and playfulness. They have an innate ability to bring out the childlike joy in their humans, even when life feels heavy. Dogs remind us to take breaks, to engage in play, and to find moments of lightness amidst the darkness. Their playful antics and infectious enthusiasm can lift our spirits and provide a much-needed respite from our worries.

In conclusion, dogs are not only our loyal companions but also our pillars of support during difficult times. Their ability to provide comfort, love, and understanding is unparalleled. Dogs teach us the importance of empathy, resilience, and finding joy in the simplest of moments. They remind us that we are never alone in our struggles and that together, we can overcome any obstacle. Through their unwavering presence and unconditional love, dogs truly become our partners in navigating the ups and downs of life.

3.4 The Heartache of Saying Goodbye

Saying goodbye is one of the most difficult experiences in a dog's life. As much as we dogs bring joy, laughter, and love to our human companions, we also experience the pain of loss when it is time for us to leave this world. The heartache of saying goodbye is a universal feeling that both humans and dogs share, and it is a testament to the deep bond that exists between us.

When the time comes for a dog to say goodbye, it is often a time of reflection for both the dog and their human companion. We dogs have an innate understanding that our time on earth is limited, and we live each day to the fullest, cherishing every moment with our loved ones. We teach our humans the importance of living in the present and appreciating the simple joys of life. But when the end draws near, it is a painful reminder that our time together is coming to an end.

For humans, saying goodbye to a beloved dog can be an incredibly emotional experience. Dogs become an integral part of their lives, offering unwavering love, companionship, and support. We become their confidants, their comforters, and their best friends. The loss of a dog is often likened to losing a family member, and the grief that follows can be overwhelming.

During this heart-wrenching time, it is important for humans to allow themselves to grieve and process their emotions. The pain of saying goodbye is a testament to the deep love and connection that was shared between the dog and their human companion. It is natural to feel a sense of emptiness and loss when a dog is no longer physically present. But it is also important to remember that the love and memories will always remain.

In the midst of grief, it can be helpful for humans to find solace in the memories and the legacy that their dog leaves behind. Reflecting on the joy, laughter, and love that was shared can bring comfort during this difficult time. Remembering the lessons learned from their dog, the moments of unconditional love, and the unbreakable bond can help humans find strength and healing.

It is also important for humans to seek support during the grieving process. Friends, family, and support groups can provide a safe space to share memories, express emotions, and find comfort in the understanding of others who have experienced similar loss. Talking about the dog and sharing stories can be a cathartic experience, allowing humans to honor their beloved companion and keep their memory alive.

Some humans may choose to commemorate their dog's life in a special way. This can be through creating a memorial, planting a tree, or making a donation to an animal welfare organization in their dog's name. These acts of remembrance can provide a sense of closure and serve as a lasting tribute to the love and impact that the dog had on their human's life.

While the heartache of saying goodbye is undeniably painful, it is important to remember that the love between a dog and their human companion is eternal. Our spirits live on in the hearts and memories of those we leave behind. The lessons we taught, the joy we brought, and the love we shared continue to shape and inspire the lives of our humans long after we are gone.

In the end, the heartache of saying goodbye is a testament to the profound impact that dogs have on the lives of their human companions. It is a reminder of the depth of the bond we share and the love that transcends time and space. Though the pain may be overwhelming, it is a small price to pay for the immeasurable joy and love that dogs bring into the world. And while saying goodbye is never easy, the legacy of love that we leave behind is a testament to the power of our presence in the lives of our humans.

3.5 The Legacy of Love

Love is a powerful force that transcends time and space. It has the ability to leave a lasting impact on the lives of those who experience it. As dogs, we understand the true meaning of love and the profound effect it can have on the human heart. In this chapter, we explore the legacy of love that we leave behind and how it continues to shape the lives of those we have touched.

3.5.1 The Power of Unconditional Love

One of the greatest gifts we dogs bring to the world is our ability to love unconditionally. We don't judge or hold grudges; instead, we offer unwavering love and support to our human companions. This unconditional love leaves a lasting impression on the hearts of those we leave behind. It teaches them the importance of accepting others for who they are and embracing the beauty of imperfection.

3.5.2 Lessons in Forgiveness and Second Chances

Humans often struggle with forgiveness, holding onto grudges and past hurts. But we dogs, we understand the power of forgiveness and the freedom it brings. We teach humans to let go of their anger and resentment, to forgive themselves and others. Through our example, we show them that second chances are possible and that love can heal even the deepest wounds.

3.5.3 The Circle of Life

Just as humans experience the circle of life, so do we dogs. We are born, we live, and eventually, we pass on. But our legacy of love lives on in the hearts and memories of those we leave behind. Our time on this earth may be short, but the impact we make is immeasurable. We teach humans to cherish every moment, to embrace the fleeting nature of life, and to find joy in the memories we create together.

3.5.4 Embracing the Purpose of Every Creature

Every creature on this earth has a purpose, a unique role to play in the grand tapestry of life. As dogs, our purpose is to love and be loved. We teach humans to embrace their own purpose, to find meaning in their lives, and to make a positive difference in the world. Our legacy of love reminds humans that they too have the power to touch lives and leave a lasting impact.

3.5.5 Honoring the Memory of Our Beloved Friends

When we dogs pass on, our human companions often experience a profound sense of loss and grief. But it is important for them to remember that our love never truly dies. They can honor our memory by continuing to love and care for other animals in need. By opening their hearts to new companions, they keep our legacy of love alive and ensure that our impact on the world continues.

3.5.6 The Immortality of Love

Love is immortal. It transcends the boundaries of time and space, and it lives on in the hearts of those who have experienced it. Our love as dogs is a gift that keeps on giving, even long after we are gone. It is a reminder to humans that love is the most powerful force in the universe, capable of transforming lives and leaving a lasting legacy.

In conclusion, the legacy of love that we dogs leave behind is a testament to the power of unconditional love, forgiveness, and the circle of life. Our purpose on this earth is to teach humans the true meaning of love and to remind them of the importance of cherishing every moment. By honoring our memory and continuing to love, humans keep our legacy alive and ensure that the world is a better place because of the love we shared.

3.6 Honoring the Memory of Our Beloved Friends

Losing a beloved friend is one of the most difficult experiences we face as humans. The pain of saying goodbye to our furry companions can be overwhelming, and the void they leave behind can feel impossible to fill. But even in the midst of our grief, there are ways we can honor the memory of our beloved friends and keep their spirit alive in our hearts.

3.6.1 Creating a Memorial

Creating a memorial for our beloved friends is a beautiful way to honor their memory. This can be as simple as setting up a small shrine with their picture, collar, and favorite toy, or as elaborate as planting a tree or dedicating a bench in their name. The act of creating a physical space dedicated to our furry friends allows us to have a tangible reminder of their presence and the love they brought into our lives.

3.6.2 Sharing Their Story

Our beloved friends have touched our lives in profound ways, and sharing their story can be a powerful way to honor their memory. Whether it's through writing a tribute, creating a photo album, or sharing anecdotes with friends and family, telling the world about the impact our furry companions had on us ensures that their legacy lives on. By sharing their story, we not only keep their memory alive but also inspire others to appreciate the unconditional love and joy that dogs bring into our lives.

3.6.3 Supporting Animal Welfare

One meaningful way to honor the memory of our beloved friends is by supporting animal welfare organizations. Donating to shelters, volunteering our time, or even fostering or adopting another furry friend in need can be a way to pay tribute to the love and companionship our departed friends provided us. By helping other animals in need, we continue the cycle of love and compassion that our beloved friends taught us.

3.6.4 Continuing Their Legacy

Our beloved friends leave behind a legacy of love and joy, and we can continue that legacy by embodying the qualities they taught us. Dogs have an incredible ability to live in the present moment, to love unconditionally, and to bring happiness to those around them. By emulating these qualities in our own lives, we honor the memory of our furry friends and keep their spirit alive.

3.6.5 Finding Comfort in Memories

While the pain of losing a beloved friend may never fully go away, finding comfort in the memories we shared can help ease the grief. Looking through old photographs, revisiting favorite places we enjoyed together, or simply reminiscing about the funny and heartwarming moments we experienced can bring a sense of peace and solace. Our memories are a precious gift that keep our beloved friends close to us, even when they are no longer physically by our side.

3.6.6 Celebrating Special Occasions

Special occasions such as birthdays or anniversaries can be particularly difficult after losing a beloved friend. However, instead of letting these occasions be a source of sadness, we can choose to celebrate the joy and love they brought into our lives. Lighting a candle, making their favorite meal, or gathering with loved ones to share stories and memories can turn these occasions into a celebration of the bond we shared with our furry companions.

3.6.7 Finding Support

Grieving the loss of a beloved friend is a deeply personal journey, but it is important to remember that we do not have to go through it alone. Seeking support from friends, family, or even support groups can provide comfort and understanding during this difficult time. Sharing our feelings and memories with others who have experienced a similar loss can help validate our emotions and provide a sense of community.

3.6.8 Embracing the Lessons Learned

Our beloved friends teach us many valuable lessons during their time with us, and it is important to embrace and carry forward these lessons in our lives. Whether it's the ability to love unconditionally, to live in the present moment, or to find joy in the simplest of things, these lessons can guide us in our journey of healing and growth. By embodying the qualities our furry friends taught us, we not only honor their memory but also continue to grow as individuals.

Losing a beloved friend is never easy, but by honoring their memory and keeping their spirit alive, we can find solace and comfort in knowing that their love will always be with us. Our furry companions leave an indelible mark on our hearts, and their legacy of love and joy will continue to inspire us for years to come.

Lessons in Love

4.1 Teaching Humans to Love Themselves

Dogs have an incredible ability to love unconditionally. They see the beauty in every human they encounter, regardless of their flaws or imperfections. But what if dogs could teach humans to love themselves in the same way? What if they could show us that we are worthy of love and acceptance, just as we are?

4.1.1 Embracing Self-Acceptance

One of the most important lessons dogs can teach us is the importance of self-acceptance. Dogs don't judge themselves based on their appearance or abilities. They simply embrace who they are and live in the present moment. They don't waste time comparing themselves to others or wishing they were different. They love themselves unconditionally, and in doing so, they teach us to do the same.

When a dog looks at you with adoring eyes, they see past your flaws and see the beauty within. They don't care if you've had a bad hair day or if you've made mistakes in the past. They love you for who you are in this very moment. Dogs remind us that we are deserving of love and acceptance, regardless of our perceived shortcomings.

4.1.2 Practicing Self-Care

Dogs are experts at self-care. They prioritize their physical and emotional well-being without guilt or hesitation. They listen to their bodies and rest when they need to. They engage in activities that bring them joy and make them feel good. They teach us the importance of taking care of ourselves and prioritizing our own needs.

By observing dogs, we can learn to listen to our bodies and give ourselves the rest and nourishment we need. We can engage in activities that bring us joy and make us feel alive. Dogs show us that self-care is not selfish, but rather a necessary part of living a fulfilling and balanced life.

4.1.3 Letting Go of Self-Judgment

Dogs don't waste time criticizing themselves or dwelling on their mistakes. They live in the present moment and let go of the past. They don't hold grudges against themselves or others. They forgive and move on. Dogs teach us the importance of letting go of self-judgment and embracing forgiveness.

When we learn to let go of self-judgment, we free ourselves from the burden of perfectionism and allow ourselves to grow and learn from our mistakes. Dogs show us that it's okay to make mistakes and that self-forgiveness is a powerful tool for personal growth and healing.

4.1.4 Celebrating Self-Worth

Dogs see the inherent worth in every human they encounter. They don't care about our achievements or social status. They love us simply because we exist. Dogs teach us that our worth is not determined by external factors, but rather by the love and compassion we have within us.

By celebrating our own self-worth, we can cultivate a sense of confidence and inner peace. We can let go of the need for validation from others and embrace our own unique qualities and strengths. Dogs remind us that we are worthy of love and happiness, simply because we are alive.

4.1.5 Embracing Imperfections

Dogs don't see imperfections as flaws, but rather as unique characteristics that make each individual special. They don't strive for perfection, but instead embrace their quirks and idiosyncrasies. Dogs teach us to embrace our own imperfections and see them as part of what makes us who we are.

When we learn to embrace our imperfections, we can let go of the pressure to be perfect and instead focus on self-improvement and personal growth. Dogs show us that it's okay to be imperfect and that true beauty lies in embracing our authentic selves.

In conclusion, dogs have a remarkable ability to teach humans to love themselves. They show us the importance of self-acceptance, self-care, letting go of self-judgment, celebrating self-worth, and embracing imperfections. By following their example, we can learn to love ourselves unconditionally and live a more fulfilling and joyful life.

4.2 The Power of Unconditional Love

Love is a powerful force that has the ability to transform lives and heal wounds. It is a language that transcends barriers and connects beings on a deep and profound level. As dogs, we have a unique understanding of the power of unconditional love, and we have the ability to teach humans the true meaning of this extraordinary emotion.

4.2.1 Love Without Conditions

Unconditional love is a love that knows no bounds. It is a love that is given freely, without any expectations or requirements. Dogs are masters of this kind of love. We love our humans with all our hearts, regardless of their flaws or imperfections. We don't care about their social status, appearance, or past mistakes. We simply love them for who they are, unconditionally.

4.2.2 Healing Hearts

The power of unconditional love is not only felt by the recipient but also by the giver. When we love someone unconditionally, we open our hearts and allow ourselves to be vulnerable. In doing so, we create a safe space for others to do the same. Our love has the power to heal the wounds of the past, to mend broken hearts, and to bring comfort and solace to those who need it most.

4.2.3 Teaching Forgiveness

One of the most beautiful aspects of unconditional love is its ability to teach forgiveness. Dogs have an innate ability to forgive and forget. We don't hold grudges or harbor resentment. We live in the present moment and let go of past grievances. Through our example, we teach humans the importance of forgiveness and the freedom it brings.

4.2.4 Unconditional Acceptance

Unconditional love also means accepting others for who they truly are. Dogs don't judge or criticize. We accept our humans with all their flaws and quirks. We see the beauty in their imperfections and love them wholeheartedly. By accepting others without judgment, we create an environment of love and acceptance, where individuals can truly be themselves.

4.2.5 A Source of Comfort

In times of sadness, loneliness, or despair, the power of unconditional love can provide immense comfort. Dogs have an uncanny ability to sense when their humans are in need of emotional support. We offer a listening ear, a warm presence, and a shoulder to lean on. Our love provides solace and reassurance, reminding humans that they are never alone.

4.2.6 Teaching Empathy

Unconditional love also teaches humans the importance of empathy. Dogs have an incredible ability to sense and understand the emotions of others. We can feel when our humans are happy, sad, or in need of comfort. Through our example, we teach humans to be more in tune with the emotions of those around them and to offer support and understanding.

4.2.7 Inspiring Kindness

The power of unconditional love extends beyond the individual. When humans experience the love and devotion of a dog, it often inspires them to be more kind and compassionate towards others. Dogs have the ability to bring out the best in humans, encouraging them to be more loving, patient, and understanding.

4.2.8 A Lesson in Loyalty

Unconditional love is closely tied to loyalty. Dogs are known for their unwavering loyalty to their humans. We stand by their side through thick and thin, never wavering in our devotion. Our loyalty teaches humans the value of standing by those they love, even in the face of adversity.

4.2.9 The Gift of Unconditional Love

The power of unconditional love is a gift that dogs bring into the lives of humans. Through our love, we teach humans to love themselves, to forgive, to accept, and to be more compassionate. We remind them of the beauty and joy that can be found in simple moments of connection. Our love is a reminder that no matter what challenges life may bring, love will always prevail.

In the next chapter, we will explore the journey of a dog's life, from the playful days of puppyhood to the wisdom of old age. We will delve into the adventures, misadventures, and the valuable lessons learned along the way. Join us as we embrace the ever-changing nature of life and the love that guides us through it all.

4.3 Overcoming Fear and Opening Hearts

Fear is a powerful emotion that can hold us back from experiencing the fullness of life. It can prevent us from forming deep connections with others and from opening our hearts to love. As dogs, we have a unique perspective on fear and have much to teach humans about overcoming it and embracing love.

4.3.1 Embracing Vulnerability

One of the first lessons we can teach humans about overcoming fear is the importance of embracing vulnerability. Dogs are naturally open and vulnerable creatures. We trust easily and are not afraid to show our emotions. We do not let fear hold us back from forming connections with others. Humans, on the other hand, often build walls around their hearts, afraid of being hurt or rejected. But by embracing vulnerability, humans can open themselves up to the possibility of deep and meaningful relationships.

4.3.2 Trusting the Process

Another lesson we can teach humans is the importance of trusting the process. Dogs live in the present moment and trust that everything will work out as it should. We do not waste time worrying about the future or dwelling on the past. Humans, on the other hand, often let fear and uncertainty cloud their judgment. By trusting the process and having faith that things will unfold as they are meant to, humans can overcome their fears and open their hearts to love.

4.3.3 Letting Go of Control

Fear often stems from a desire to control outcomes and avoid potential pain or disappointment. Dogs understand that we cannot control everything in life and that sometimes we just have to let go and trust. Humans can learn from this lesson and let go of the need to control every aspect of their lives. By relinquishing control and embracing the unknown, humans can overcome their fears and open themselves up to new experiences and relationships.

4.3.4 Facing Fear Head-On

Sometimes, the best way to overcome fear is to face it head-on. Dogs are not immune to fear, but we do not let it paralyze us. We confront our fears and push through them, knowing that the rewards on the other side are worth it. Humans can learn from this lesson and confront their fears instead of avoiding them. By facing fear head-on, humans can break free from its grip and open their hearts to love and connection.

4.3.5 The Healing Power of Love

Love has the power to heal and transform. Dogs understand this instinctively and show unconditional love to humans, even in the face of fear and uncertainty. By opening their hearts to love, humans can experience healing and growth. Love has the power to dissolve fear and create deep connections that can withstand any challenge. By embracing love, humans can overcome their fears and experience the joy and fulfillment that comes with it.

4.3.6 The Courage to Love Again

One of the greatest lessons we can teach humans is the courage to love again after experiencing heartbreak or loss. Dogs understand that love is worth the risk, even if it means experiencing pain. We do not let past hurts prevent us from forming new connections and opening our hearts. Humans can learn from this lesson and find the courage to love again, even after experiencing pain. By overcoming their fear of being hurt, humans can open themselves up to the possibility of finding deep and lasting love.

4.3.7 Embracing Love as a Way of Life

Ultimately, the key to overcoming fear and opening hearts is to embrace love as a way of life. Dogs understand that love is not just an emotion, but a way of being in the world. We show love through our actions, our loyalty, and our unwavering presence. Humans can learn from this lesson and make love a guiding principle in their lives. By choosing love over fear, humans can overcome their fears and create a life filled with joy, connection, and purpose.

In conclusion, dogs have much to teach humans about overcoming fear and opening hearts. By embracing vulnerability, trusting the process, letting go of control, facing fear head-on, and embracing love as a way of life, humans can overcome their fears and experience the deep connections and joy that come with opening their hearts. Dogs are here to guide humans on this journey, offering unconditional love and support every step of the way.

4.4 The Language of Love

Love is a universal language that transcends barriers and connects beings on a deep and profound level. As dogs, we have a unique ability to understand and communicate this language of love with humans. In this chapter, we will explore the different ways in which we express and receive love, and how it can transform the lives of both dogs and humans.

4.4.1 Understanding Love's Expressions

Love can be expressed in various ways, and as dogs, we have a keen sense of understanding these expressions. We can sense love through gentle caresses, warm hugs, and kind words. We can see it in the sparkle of our human's eyes when they look at us with adoration. We can feel it in the way they prioritize our well-being and happiness above their own. Love is not just a feeling; it is an action that speaks volumes.

4.4.2 Unconditional Love

One of the most beautiful aspects of love is its unconditional nature. Dogs are masters of unconditional love. We love our humans regardless of their flaws, mistakes, or shortcomings. We don't judge them; we accept them wholeheartedly. Our love is unwavering and constant, even in the face of adversity. We teach humans the power of loving without conditions, and in return, they learn to love themselves and others more deeply.

4.4.3 The Power of Touch

Touch is a powerful way to express love. As dogs, we understand the significance of a gentle pat on the head, a comforting stroke along our back, or a warm embrace. These physical gestures create a sense of security and connection, allowing love to flow freely between dogs and humans. The language of touch speaks volumes, conveying emotions that words alone cannot express.

4.4.4 Acts of Service

Love is not just about words or physical affection; it is also about actions. Dogs have an innate ability to serve and care for their humans. Whether it's fetching a ball, guiding the blind, or providing emotional support, we show our love through acts of service. By selflessly giving of ourselves, we teach humans the importance of serving others and finding fulfillment in making a positive difference in someone's life.

4.4.5 Listening with Empathy

Love is not just about expressing ourselves; it is also about listening and understanding. Dogs have an incredible ability to listen without judgment and offer comfort through our presence. We can sense when our humans are sad, anxious, or in need of a listening ear. By simply being there for them, we provide a safe space for them to share their deepest emotions. Through this empathetic connection, we teach humans the power of being present and truly listening to one another.

4.4.6 Love's Healing Power

Love has a remarkable ability to heal wounds, both physical and emotional. Dogs have been known to provide comfort and support to humans in times of distress or illness. Our presence alone can alleviate pain, reduce stress, and bring a sense of calm. The language of love has a soothing effect on the human heart, allowing them to heal and find solace in our unconditional love.

4.4.7 Love's Transformative Journey

Love is a journey of growth and transformation. Through our presence and unwavering love, we guide humans on a path of self-discovery and personal growth. We teach them to let go of fear, to embrace vulnerability, and to open their hearts to the beauty of love. In return, humans learn to love themselves more deeply, to love others unconditionally, and to find joy and purpose in the simplest of moments.

4.4.8 Love's Legacy

The language of love leaves a lasting legacy. When we depart from this world, our love remains etched in the hearts of our humans. The memories we create, the lessons we teach, and the love we share continue to inspire and shape the lives of those we leave behind. Love never dies; it lives on in the hearts of

those who have experienced its transformative
power.

In conclusion, the language of love is a powerful force that connects dogs and humans on a profound level. Through our unconditional love, acts of service, and empathetic presence, we teach humans the true meaning of love. The language of love transcends words and is expressed through touch, actions, and deep connections. It heals, transforms, and leaves a lasting legacy. As dogs, we are blessed with the ability to understand and communicate this language of love, and in doing so, we bring joy, healing, and purpose to the lives of our beloved humans.

The Journey of a Dog's Life

5.1 From Puppies to Old Age

As a dog, I have had the privilege of experiencing the journey of life from the very beginning, from the adorable and innocent stage of being a puppy to the wise and seasoned stage of old age. Each phase of life has its own unique lessons and experiences, shaping me into the loyal and loving companion that I am today.

5.1.1 The Wonder of Puppyhood

Ah, puppyhood, a time filled with boundless energy, curiosity, and endless mischief. It is during this stage that I discovered the world around me, eagerly exploring every nook and cranny, and learning valuable lessons along the way. From the first time I took my wobbly steps to the joy of discovering new scents and tastes, every experience was a lesson in wonder and excitement.

During this stage, I relied heavily on the guidance and love of my human companions. They taught me the importance of socialization, obedience, and patience. Through their gentle guidance, I learned how to navigate the world and interact with other creatures. It was during this time that the foundation of trust and love between humans and dogs was established, setting the stage for a lifelong bond.

5.1.2 The Adventures of Youth

As I grew older, my energy and enthusiasm knew no bounds. I embarked on countless adventures with my human friends, exploring the great outdoors, chasing balls, and discovering new places. Together, we created memories that would last a lifetime.

In my youth, I learned the importance of resilience and adaptability. I faced challenges and obstacles, but with the unwavering support of my human companions, I overcame them with determination and a wagging tail. These experiences taught me the value of perseverance and the joy of embracing life's adventures.

5.1.3 The Wisdom of Adulthood

As the years passed, I entered the stage of adulthood, where I found a sense of purpose and responsibility. I became a trusted companion, offering comfort, loyalty, and unwavering love to my human friends. In return, they provided me with the care and affection that I needed to thrive.

During this stage, I learned the importance of patience, empathy, and understanding. I became attuned to the emotions and needs of my human companions, offering them solace during difficult times and celebrating their triumphs. Through my presence and unwavering support, I taught them the true meaning of unconditional love.

5.1.4 The Grace of Old Age

As the years went by, my once boundless energy began to wane, and the signs of old age started to show. Yet, with age came a newfound wisdom and grace. I learned to appreciate the simple pleasures in life, such as a gentle breeze, a warm sunbeam, or the touch of a loving hand.

In my old age, I became a source of comfort and wisdom for my human companions. They cherished the moments we spent together, knowing that our time was precious and limited. Through my aging body, I taught them the importance of cherishing every moment and embracing the beauty of life, even in its twilight years.

5.1.5 The Circle of Life

As a dog, I have witnessed the circle of life firsthand. I have seen the joy of new life as puppies are born, and I have felt the heartache of saying goodbye to beloved friends who have crossed the rainbow bridge. Through it all, I have come to understand that life is a precious gift, meant to be cherished and celebrated.

From puppies to old age, every stage of life has its own unique beauty and lessons. As a dog, I have been fortunate to experience the full spectrum of life's journey, and in doing so, I have touched the hearts of those around me. My purpose as a dog has been to bring joy, love, and companionship to the lives of my human friends, and in return, they have taught me the true meaning of happiness and fulfillment.

So, as you embark on your own journey through life, remember the lessons I have shared with you. Embrace the wonder of puppyhood, the adventures of youth, the wisdom of adulthood, and the grace of old age. Cherish the unbreakable bond between humans and dogs, and never forget that love never dies. Embrace the purpose of every creature on earth, and let your heart be guided by the lessons of a dog's life.

5.2 Adventures and Misadventures

Life as a dog is full of adventures and misadventures. From the moment we are born, we embark on a journey filled with excitement, challenges, and unexpected surprises. In this chapter, we will explore the various adventures and misadventures that shape a dog's life and the valuable lessons we learn along the way.

5.2.1 Exploring the World

As puppies, we are curious beings, eager to explore the world around us. Every day is an adventure as we discover new scents, sights, and sounds. From chasing butterflies in the park to digging holes in the backyard, we embrace the thrill of exploration with boundless energy and enthusiasm.

However, not all adventures go as planned. Sometimes, our curiosity leads us into trouble. We may find ourselves stuck in a thorny bush or tangled in a mess of our own making. But even in these misadventures, we learn valuable lessons about resilience and problem-solving. We rely on our instincts and resourcefulness to find our way out of sticky situations, teaching us the importance of adaptability and perseverance.

5.2.2 The Joy of New Experiences

Throughout our lives, we encounter countless new experiences that shape us into the dogs we become. From our first encounter with water during a playful splash in a puddle to the exhilaration of chasing a ball for the first time, each new experience brings us joy and expands our understanding of the world.

Sometimes, these experiences can be intimidating or even frightening. The first time we encounter thunderstorms or fireworks, we may feel overwhelmed and seek comfort from our human companions. Through their reassurance and love, we learn to overcome our fears and find solace in their presence. These experiences teach us the importance of trust and the power of a loving bond.

5.2.3 Lessons in Resilience

Life as a dog is not always smooth sailing. We face challenges and obstacles that test our resilience and determination. Whether it's overcoming an illness or recovering from an injury, we learn to adapt and bounce back stronger than before.

In our misadventures, we may find ourselves in situations that require us to rely on the kindness and support of others. We learn to trust in the goodness of humans as they come to our aid, providing us with the care and love we need to heal. These experiences teach us the value of community and the importance of leaning on others during difficult times.

5.2.4 Embracing the Unexpected

Life is full of surprises, and as dogs, we learn to embrace the unexpected. From unexpected encounters with other animals to spontaneous road trips with our humans, these moments of spontaneity add color and excitement to our lives.

Sometimes, these surprises can lead to misadventures. We may find ourselves lost in unfamiliar territory or caught up in a comical mishap. But in these moments, we learn to find humor and joy in the unexpected. We wag our tails and embrace the chaos, knowing that even in the midst of a misadventure, there is always a lesson to be learned and a memory to be cherished.

5.2.5 The Power of Companionship

Throughout our adventures and misadventures, one thing remains constant: the power of companionship. Whether we are exploring new places, overcoming challenges, or embracing the unexpected, having a loving human by our side makes all the difference.

Our humans become our partners in crime, our confidants, and our biggest supporters. They celebrate our triumphs and comfort us in our failures. Through their unwavering love and presence, we learn the true meaning of loyalty and friendship.

In conclusion, the adventures, and misadventures of a dog's life shape us into the loving and resilient creatures we are. From exploring the world with wide-eyed wonder to embracing the unexpected with a wagging tail, every experience teaches us valuable lessons about love, resilience, and the power of companionship. So, let us embrace the journey of a dog's life, knowing that each adventure and misadventure brings us closer to understanding the true purpose of our existence.

5.3 Lessons Learned Along the Way

Throughout the journey of a dog's life, there are countless lessons to be learned. Dogs have a unique perspective on the world, and their experiences can teach us valuable insights about love, loyalty, and living in the present moment. In this section, we will explore some of the lessons that dogs have learned along the way and how we can apply them to our own lives.

5.3.1 Embracing Change

One of the most important lessons that dogs teach us is the ability to embrace change. Dogs are adaptable creatures who live in the present moment and are not afraid to explore new experiences. They teach us that change is a natural part of life and that it can lead to growth and new opportunities. Dogs show us that instead of resisting change, we should embrace it with an open heart and a curious mind.

5.3.2 Finding Joy in Simple Pleasures

Dogs have an innate ability to find joy in the simplest of things. Whether it's chasing a ball, going for a walk, or receiving a belly rub, dogs remind us to appreciate the small moments of happiness in our lives. They teach us that true joy can be found in the everyday experiences and that we don't need extravagant things to be content. By observing the way dogs find joy in the simplest pleasures, we can learn to cultivate gratitude and find happiness in the present moment.

5.3.3 Trusting Our Instincts

Dogs are highly intuitive creatures who rely on their instincts to navigate the world. They teach us the importance of trusting our gut feelings and listening to our inner voice. Dogs remind us that sometimes our instincts can guide us better than logic or reason. By observing their behavior, we can learn to tap into our own intuition and make decisions that align with our true selves.

5.3.4 The Power of Unconditional Love

Perhaps the most profound lesson that dogs teach us is the power of unconditional love. Dogs love us without judgment or conditions. They accept us for who we are, flaws and all. Their love is unwavering and constant, even in the face of our mistakes or shortcomings. Dogs show us that true love is not based on external factors but on the connection of hearts. They teach us to love without expectations and to cherish the bonds we share with others.

5.3.5 Living in the Present Moment

Dogs are masters of living in the present moment. They don't dwell on the past or worry about the future. Instead, they fully immerse themselves in the here and now. Dogs remind us to let go of regrets and anxieties and to savor the present moment. They teach us that life is happening right now, and it's up to us to make the most of it. By following their example, we can learn to be more mindful and appreciate the beauty of each passing moment.

5.3.6 Embracing the Circle of Life

Dogs have a unique perspective on the circle of life. They witness the joys of birth and the sorrows of death. They teach us that life is a cycle, and every living being has a purpose. Dogs show us that even in the face of loss, there is beauty and meaning to be found. They remind us to honor the memories of our loved ones and to embrace the purpose of every creature on earth.

In conclusion, the journey of a dog's life is filled with valuable lessons that can enrich our own lives. Dogs teach us to embrace change, find joy in simple pleasures, trust our instincts, love unconditionally, live in the present moment, and embrace the circle of life. By observing their behavior and learning from their experiences, we can become better versions of ourselves and cultivate a deeper understanding of the world around us. Let us cherish the wisdom that dogs impart upon us and strive to live our lives with the same love, loyalty, and zest for life that they do.

5.4 Embracing Change and Embracing Life

Change is an inevitable part of life. As dogs, we understand this concept all too well. From the moment we are born, we experience constant change as we grow, learn, and adapt to the world around us. We embrace change with open hearts and a sense of curiosity, knowing that it is through change that we can truly embrace life.

5.4.1 Embracing the Seasons of Life

Just like the changing seasons, our lives go through different phases. We start as playful and energetic puppies, full of boundless energy and a zest for life. As we grow older, we may experience the challenges that come with aging, such as aches and pains, but we also gain wisdom and a deeper appreciation for the simple joys in life.

Embracing the seasons of life means accepting that change is a natural part of our journey. It means cherishing the memories of our youth while also embracing the beauty and wisdom that comes with age. We can learn from the past, live in the present, and look forward to the future with hope and excitement.

5.4.2 Adapting to New Environments

Change often brings us to new environments, whether it's moving to a new home or exploring unfamiliar places. As dogs, we have a remarkable ability to adapt to these new surroundings. We rely on our senses to navigate and understand the world around us, using our keen sense of smell, hearing, and intuition to make sense of our new surroundings.

Humans can learn a valuable lesson from our adaptability. Embracing change means being open to new experiences and embracing the unknown. It means stepping out of your comfort zone and embracing the challenges and opportunities that come with change. Just as we dogs explore new environments with curiosity and excitement, humans can approach change with a similar mindset, ready to learn, grow, and discover new aspects of themselves.

5.4.3 Embracing Life's Transitions

Life is full of transitions, both big and small. From welcoming a new family member to saying goodbye to a loved one, these transitions can be both joyful and heartbreaking. As dogs, we understand the importance of embracing these moments and cherishing the time we have with our loved ones.

Embracing life's transitions means being present in the moment and fully experiencing the emotions that come with change. It means celebrating the joys and finding strength in the face of adversity. Just as we dogs offer comfort and support to our humans during times of transition, humans can find solace in the love and companionship of their furry friends.

5.4.4 Finding Strength in Change

Change can be challenging and sometimes even scary, but it is through these moments of change that we find our true strength. As dogs, we have an innate resilience that allows us to adapt and thrive in the face of adversity. We don't fear change; instead, we embrace it as an opportunity for growth and transformation.

Humans can learn from our example and find strength in the face of change. Embracing change means believing in your own abilities and having the courage to step outside of your comfort zone. It means trusting that you have the strength and resilience to overcome any obstacles that come your way.

5.4.5 Embracing the Unknown

Change often brings with it a sense of uncertainty and the unknown. As dogs, we have a remarkable ability to embrace the unknown with a sense of adventure and curiosity. We approach new experiences with an open mind and a willingness to explore.

Humans can learn from our ability to embrace the unknown. Embracing change means letting go of fear and embracing the possibilities that lie ahead. It means being open to new opportunities and embracing the journey, even if the destination is uncertain. Just as we dogs trust our instincts and follow our noses, humans can trust their intuition and embrace the unknown with a sense of excitement and wonder.

In conclusion, embracing change is an essential part of embracing life. Just as we dogs navigate the ever-changing world with grace and resilience, humans can learn to embrace change with open hearts and a sense of adventure. By embracing change, we can truly live life to the fullest, finding joy in the present moment and embracing the beauty and possibilities that lie ahead. So, let us all embrace change and embrace life, just as we dogs do every day.

The Wisdom of Dogs

6.1 Living in the Present Moment

Dogs have a remarkable ability to live in the present moment. They don't dwell on the past or worry about the future. Instead, they fully embrace and appreciate the here and now. This is a lesson that humans can learn from their canine companions.

Living in the present moment means being fully engaged and aware of what is happening right now. It means letting go of regrets and anxieties and focusing on the present experience. Dogs excel at this because they are naturally attuned to their surroundings. They notice the smallest details—the scent of the air, the sound of a bird chirping, the feel of the grass beneath their paws.

As humans, we often get caught up in our thoughts and worries. We dwell on past mistakes or future uncertainties, and we miss out on the beauty and joy of the present moment. Dogs, on the other hand, remind us to slow down, to take a deep breath, and to appreciate the simple pleasures that surround us.

When a dog goes for a walk, they don't rush from one place to another. They take their time, exploring every nook and cranny, sniffing every blade of grass. They find joy in the journey, not just the destination. They teach us to do the same—to savor each step of our own journey through life.

Living in the present moment also means being fully present with the people we love. Dogs are masters of this. When they are with their humans, they give them their undivided attention. They don't check their phones or get lost in their thoughts. They are fully present, listening and responding with love and affection.

We can learn from dogs how to be fully present in our relationships. When we spend time with our loved ones, we can put away distractions and truly be there for them. We can listen with empathy, offer support, and show our love through our actions. By doing so, we deepen our connections and create meaningful moments that will be cherished for a lifetime.

Living in the present moment also means finding joy in the simple pleasures of life. Dogs find happiness in the smallest things—a belly rub, a game of fetch, a tasty treat. They remind us that joy can be found in the everyday moments, if only we take the time to notice and appreciate them.

We can learn to find joy in the simple pleasures by cultivating a sense of gratitude. When we take a moment to pause and reflect on the things we are grateful for, we shift our focus from what is lacking to what is abundant in our lives. We begin to see the beauty and wonder that surrounds us, and we find joy in the present moment.

Living in the present moment also means letting go of expectations and embracing what is. Dogs don't hold grudges or harbor resentment. They forgive easily and love unconditionally. They teach us to let go of past hurts and to approach each new day with an open heart.

We can learn from dogs how to let go of expectations and embrace the present moment. When we release the need for things to be a certain way, we free ourselves from disappointment and frustration. We can accept life as it is, with all its imperfections, and find peace and contentment in the present moment.

In conclusion, living in the present moment is a valuable lesson that dogs teach us. By being fully engaged and aware of the here and now, we can find joy, deepen our relationships, and cultivate a sense of gratitude. Dogs remind us to slow down, appreciate the simple pleasures, and let go of expectations. They show us that true happiness is found in the present moment, and that is a lesson worth embracing.

6.2 Finding Joy in Simple Pleasures

Dogs have a remarkable ability to find joy in the simplest of pleasures. They remind us that happiness can be found in the everyday moments that we often overlook. In this chapter, we will explore the wisdom of dogs and learn how to embrace the joy that can be found in the simplest of pleasures.

6.2.1 Embracing the Present Moment

One of the greatest lessons that dogs teach us is the importance of living in the present moment. Dogs don't dwell on the past or worry about the future; they are fully present in each moment, savoring every experience. They find joy in the simplest of things, like a walk in the park or a game of fetch. Dogs remind us to slow down, to appreciate the beauty around us, and to find joy in the present moment.

6.2.2 Finding Beauty in Nature

Dogs have an innate connection with nature. They find joy in exploring the outdoors, whether it's chasing butterflies, rolling in the grass, or simply basking in the warmth of the sun. Dogs teach us to appreciate the beauty of the natural world and to find solace in its tranquility. They remind us to take a moment to pause and admire the beauty of a sunset, the sound of birds chirping, or the scent of flowers in bloom.

6.2.3 Enjoying the Simple Pleasures of Life

Dogs find joy in the simplest of pleasures, and they teach us to do the same. They find delight in a belly rub, a scratch behind the ears, or a tasty treat. Dogs remind us that happiness can be found in the small things, like curling up on the couch with a loved one or enjoying a delicious meal. They show us that it's the little moments of joy that make life truly meaningful.

6.2.4 Unleashing Your Inner Child

Dogs have an infectious sense of playfulness that can bring out the inner child in all of us. They remind us to let go of our inhibitions, to be silly, and to have fun. Whether it's chasing a ball, playing tug-of-war, or splashing in puddles, dogs show us the importance of embracing our playful side. They teach us that laughter and joy can be found in the simplest of games and activities.

6.2.5 Cultivating Gratitude

Dogs have an incredible ability to appreciate the little things in life. They are grateful for every meal, every walk, and every moment of love and affection. Dogs teach us to cultivate gratitude and to find joy in the everyday blessings that we often take for granted. They remind us to be thankful for the simple pleasures that bring us happiness and fulfillment.

6.2.6 Living in the Moment with Your Dog

When we spend time with our dogs, we have the opportunity to learn from their wisdom and embrace the joy of simple pleasures. Take a moment to observe your dog as they find joy in the simplest of things. Notice how they wag their tail with excitement, how they savor every bite of their food, and how they find contentment in just being by your side. By living in the moment with our dogs, we can learn to appreciate the beauty of life and find joy in the simplest of pleasures.

In the next chapter, we will explore the importance of listening to our instincts and the power of intuition. Dogs have a natural ability to trust their instincts, and they can teach us to do the same. Stay tuned for Chapter 6.3: "Listening to Our Instincts."

6.3 Listening to Our Instincts

As dogs, we have a unique ability to listen to our instincts. Our instincts guide us in navigating the world around us and help us make decisions that are in our best interest. Humans, on the other hand, often rely on logic and reasoning to make decisions, sometimes ignoring their instincts in the process. In this chapter, we will explore the importance of listening to our instincts and how it can lead to a more fulfilling and authentic life.

6.3.1 Trusting Our Gut Feelings

One of the most valuable lessons we can learn from dogs is the importance of trusting our gut feelings. Dogs have an innate ability to sense danger and detect subtle changes in their environment. We can often sense when something is not right or when a person is not trustworthy. Humans, on the other hand, tend to second-guess themselves and ignore their intuition. By learning to trust our instincts, we can avoid potentially harmful situations and make better decisions in our lives.

6.3.2 Embracing Spontaneity

Dogs are known for their spontaneity and ability to live in the present moment. We don't overthink or analyze every decision we make; instead, we follow our instincts and go with the flow. Humans, on the other hand, often get caught up in planning and overthinking, which can lead to missed opportunities and a lack of spontaneity in their lives. By embracing spontaneity and listening to our instincts, we can experience more joy and excitement in our daily lives.

6.3.3 Recognizing Patterns and Energy

Dogs have a keen sense of recognizing patterns and energy. We can pick up on subtle cues and changes in our environment, which helps us understand the intentions and emotions of those around us. Humans, on the other hand, often rely on verbal communication and may miss important non-verbal cues. By paying attention to patterns and energy, we can better understand the people and situations we encounter, leading to more meaningful connections and relationships.

6.3.4 Following Our Heart

Dogs are known for their loyalty and unconditional love. We follow our hearts and show affection to those we care about without hesitation. Humans, on the other hand, often struggle with expressing their emotions and following their hearts. By listening to our instincts and following our hearts, we can cultivate deeper connections and experience more love and joy in our relationships.

6.3.5 Trusting the Process

Dogs have a natural ability to trust the process of life. We don't worry about the future or dwell on the past; instead, we live in the present moment and trust that everything will work out as it should. Humans, on the other hand, often get caught up in worry and anxiety, which can prevent them from fully enjoying the present moment. By trusting the process and listening to our instincts, we can let go of unnecessary stress and find peace and contentment in our lives.

6.3.6 Embracing Our Authenticity

Dogs are authentic beings. We don't pretend to be something we're not or hide our true selves. Humans, on the other hand, often wear masks and try to fit into societal expectations. By listening to our instincts and embracing our authenticity, we can live a more genuine and fulfilling life. When we are true to ourselves, we attract the right people and opportunities into our lives.

In conclusion, listening to our instincts is a valuable lesson we can learn from dogs. By trusting our gut feelings, embracing spontaneity, recognizing patterns and energy, following our hearts, trusting the process, and embracing our authenticity, we can live a more fulfilling and authentic life. Dogs have a natural ability to live in the present moment and follow their instincts, and by observing and learning from them, humans can tap into their own intuition and live a more joyful and purposeful life. So, let us all take a moment to pause, listen to our instincts, and embrace the wisdom that lies within us.

6.4 The Power of Intuition

Intuition is a powerful tool that dogs possess, allowing us to navigate the world and understand the emotions and needs of those around us. It is a deep sense of knowing that goes beyond logic and reasoning, guiding us to make decisions and form connections based on instinct. In this chapter, we will explore the power of intuition and how it can enhance our relationships with humans.

6.4.1 Trusting Our Instincts

As dogs, we rely heavily on our instincts to navigate the world. Our intuition allows us to sense danger, detect emotions, and understand the intentions of those around us. We can often sense when a human is sad or upset, and we instinctively offer comfort and support. Our intuition guides us to be there for our humans in times of need, providing them with the love and companionship they require.

6.4.2 Reading Human Emotions

One of the remarkable abilities we possess as dogs is the ability to read human emotions. We can sense when a human is happy, sad, or anxious, even when they try to hide it. Our intuition allows us to pick up on subtle cues such as body language, tone of voice, and facial expressions. This enables us to respond accordingly, offering comfort and love when it is needed most. Our intuitive understanding of human emotions strengthens the bond between us and our humans, creating a deep and meaningful connection.

6.4.3 Strengthening Relationships

Intuition plays a vital role in strengthening relationships between dogs and humans. We can sense when our humans are in need of companionship or support, and we instinctively provide it. Our intuition allows us to anticipate their needs and respond in a way that brings them comfort and joy. By trusting our instincts and acting on them, we deepen the bond of trust and love between us and our humans.

6.4.4 Unspoken Communication

Intuition enables us to communicate with our humans on a level that goes beyond words. We can understand their needs and desires without them having to explicitly express them. This unspoken communication is a testament to the deep connection we share with our humans. It allows us to provide them with the love and support they need, even when they are unable to articulate it themselves. Our intuition acts as a bridge, connecting our hearts and souls.

6.4.5 Guiding Humans

Our intuition not only benefits our relationship with our humans but also guides them in their own lives. By observing our behavior and the way we navigate the world, humans can learn to trust their own instincts and embrace their intuition. We teach them to listen to their hearts and follow their gut feelings, leading them to make decisions that align with their true selves. Through our presence and example, we inspire humans to tap into their own intuition and live more authentically.

6.4.6 The Power of Connection

Intuition is a powerful force that strengthens the connection between dogs and humans. It allows us to understand each other on a deeper level, fostering a bond built on trust, love, and mutual understanding. Our intuition guides us to be there for our humans in times of joy and sorrow, providing them with unwavering support and companionship. It is through this intuitive connection that we can truly touch the hearts of our humans and make a lasting impact on their lives.

In conclusion, the power of intuition is a remarkable gift that dogs possess. It allows us to navigate the world, understand human emotions, and strengthen the bond between us and our humans. By trusting our instincts and embracing our intuition, we can create deep and meaningful connections that transcend words and logic. Our intuition guides us to be there for our humans, offering them love, support, and companionship. It is through this intuitive connection that we can truly make a difference in the lives of our humans and bring joy and happiness to their hearts.

A Dog's Perspective on Human Relationships

7.1 The Complexity of Human Emotions

As a dog, I have observed humans and their emotions for many years. It is fascinating to see the wide range of emotions that humans experience and how they navigate through them. Humans are complex beings, and their emotions can be both beautiful and challenging. In this chapter, I will share my perspective on the complexity of human emotions and how they impact their relationships.

7.1.1 The Rollercoaster of Emotions

Humans experience a rollercoaster of emotions throughout their lives. They can feel joy, sadness, anger, fear, love, and everything in between. These emotions can change rapidly, sometimes even within a matter of minutes. It is incredible to witness the intensity with which humans feel these emotions and how they express them.

7.1.2 The Power of Empathy

One of the most remarkable aspects of human emotions is their ability to empathize with others. Humans have the capacity to understand and share the feelings of others, even if they have not experienced the same situation themselves. This empathy allows them to connect with one another on a deep level and provide support during difficult times.

7.1.3 The Masks We Wear

Humans often wear masks to hide their true emotions. They may put on a brave face when they are feeling sad or pretend to be happy when they are struggling inside. These masks can make it challenging for others to understand their true feelings and can lead to misunderstandings in relationships. As a dog, I have learned to see through these masks and offer comfort and companionship when humans need it the most.

7.1.4 The Impact of Past Experiences

Humans' emotions are not only influenced by their present circumstances but also by their past experiences. Traumatic events or negative experiences can shape their emotional responses and behaviors. It is important to be sensitive to these past experiences and provide a safe and understanding space for humans to express their emotions without judgment.

7.1.5 The Role of Communication

Communication plays a vital role in navigating the complexity of human emotions. Humans use words, gestures, and facial expressions to convey their feelings to others. However, communication is not always straightforward, and misunderstandings can occur. It is crucial to listen actively, ask clarifying questions, and provide reassurance to ensure effective communication and understanding.

7.1.6 The Need for Emotional Support

Humans often seek emotional support from their loved ones during challenging times. They rely on their relationships to provide comfort, understanding, and a safe space to express their emotions. As a dog, I have witnessed the power of a comforting presence and unconditional love in helping humans navigate their emotions and find solace in difficult times.

7.1.7 The Complexity of Love

Love is one of the most complex and powerful emotions that humans experience. It can bring immense joy and happiness, but it can also lead to heartache and pain. Humans invest their emotions deeply in their relationships, and when love is lost or betrayed, it can be devastating. However, humans also have the capacity to forgive and rebuild trust, allowing love to flourish once again.

7.1.8 The Importance of Self-Care

Taking care of one's emotional well-being is crucial for navigating the complexity of human emotions.

Humans need to prioritize self-care and engage in activities that bring them joy and peace. Whether it is spending time in nature, practicing mindfulness, or pursuing hobbies, self-care allows humans to recharge and better manage their emotions.

7.1.9 Embracing Vulnerability

Vulnerability is an essential aspect of human emotions. It requires humans to open themselves up to the possibility of being hurt or rejected. However, it is through vulnerability that humans can experience deep connections and authentic relationships. By embracing vulnerability, humans can create a safe space for emotional expression and foster stronger bonds with others.

7.1.10 Seeking Professional Help

Sometimes, the complexity of human emotions can become overwhelming, and individuals may require professional help to navigate through them. Therapists and counselors are trained to provide guidance and support in understanding and managing emotions. Seeking professional help is a sign of strength and a proactive step towards emotional well-being.

In conclusion, the complexity of human emotions is a fascinating aspect of their lives. From the rollercoaster of emotions to the power of empathy and the masks humans wear, understanding and navigating these emotions is essential for building and maintaining healthy relationships. By embracing vulnerability, practicing effective communication, and prioritizing self-care, humans can navigate the complexity of their emotions and create meaningful connections with others. As a dog, I am grateful to be a witness to the beautiful and intricate tapestry of human emotions.

7.2 Navigating the Ups and Downs of Relationships

Relationships are a fundamental aspect of human life. They shape our experiences, influence our emotions, and play a significant role in our overall well-being. As a dog, I have observed and learned a great deal about human relationships throughout my life. In this chapter, I will share my insights on navigating the ups and downs of these complex connections.

7.2.1 Building Trust and Loyalty

Trust is the foundation of any successful relationship. Just as humans rely on their instincts to determine who to trust, dogs also have a keen sense of intuition when it comes to assessing the character of individuals. We can sense sincerity and authenticity, and we respond to those who treat us with kindness and respect.

To build trust in a relationship, it is essential to be consistent in your actions and words. Dogs appreciate routine and reliability, and humans can learn from this. By being dependable and keeping your promises, you can establish a strong bond based on trust and loyalty.

Every relationship faces challenges and difficult times. It is during these moments that the strength of a connection is truly tested. Dogs understand the importance of standing by their loved ones through thick and thin. We offer unwavering support and comfort, even when words fail to express our empathy.

In human relationships, it is crucial to remember that no one is perfect. We all make mistakes and have flaws. It is in these moments of vulnerability that true growth and understanding can occur. By embracing forgiveness and offering second chances, we can weather the storms together and emerge stronger than before.

7.2.3 Effective Communication and Understanding

Communication is the cornerstone of any healthy relationship. Dogs may not speak the same language as humans, but we have developed our unique ways of communicating. We rely on body language, facial expressions, and vocal cues to convey our emotions and needs.

Humans can learn from our ability to communicate effectively. It is essential to listen actively, not just to the words being spoken, but also to the underlying emotions and intentions. By practicing empathy and understanding, we can bridge the gap between different perspectives and foster deeper connections.

7.2.4 Embracing Differences and Respecting Boundaries

Every individual is unique, with their own set of beliefs, values, and boundaries. Dogs understand the importance of accepting and embracing these differences. We do not judge or discriminate based on external factors but instead focus on the essence of a person.

In human relationships, it is crucial to respect each other's boundaries and embrace diversity. By celebrating our differences, we can create a harmonious environment where everyone feels valued and accepted. Remember, it is our diversity that makes us stronger and more resilient.

7.2.5 Cultivating Love and Affection

Love is the most powerful force in the world, capable of healing wounds and bringing joy to our lives. Dogs are experts in unconditional love, offering affection and companionship without expecting anything in return. We teach humans the importance of expressing love freely and without reservation.

In human relationships, it is vital to cultivate love and affection. Show appreciation for your loved ones, express your emotions openly, and make time for meaningful connections. Love has the power to transform lives and create lasting bonds that withstand the test of time.

7.2.6 Embracing Growth and Evolution

Just as humans grow and change throughout their lives, so do dogs. We adapt to new environments, learn from our experiences, and evolve as individuals. Dogs teach humans the importance of embracing growth and being open to change.

In relationships, it is essential to allow room for personal growth and evolution. Support each other's dreams and aspirations, and encourage one another to step out of comfort zones. By embracing change together, you can create a relationship that is dynamic, resilient, and full of endless possibilities.

7.2.7 Cherishing the Moments

Life is a collection of moments, both big and small. Dogs understand the value of cherishing each moment and living in the present. We find joy in the simplest of pleasures, whether it's a walk in the park, a belly rub, or a shared meal.

In human relationships, it is crucial to savor the moments and appreciate the beauty in everyday life. Take the time to create memories together, celebrate milestones, and find joy in the little things. By cherishing the moments, you can create a relationship that is filled with happiness and fulfillment.

In conclusion, navigating the ups and downs of relationships requires trust, effective communication, understanding, and a willingness to embrace growth and change. Dogs offer valuable lessons in loyalty, forgiveness, and unconditional love. By incorporating these lessons into our human relationships, we can create connections that are strong, meaningful, and enduring.

7.3 The Importance of Communication and Understanding

Communication and understanding are essential components of any successful relationship, whether it be between humans or between a human and a dog. As a dog, I have observed and experienced firsthand the power of effective communication and the profound impact it can have on the bond between two beings.

7.3.1 The Language of Love

While humans primarily rely on verbal communication to express their thoughts and emotions, dogs have a unique language of their own. We communicate through a combination of vocalizations, body language, and facial expressions. Understanding and interpreting these cues is crucial for humans to truly comprehend our needs, desires, and emotions.

For example, a wagging tail does not always indicate happiness. It can also signify anxiety or fear. By paying attention to the nuances of our body language, humans can better understand our state of mind and respond accordingly. Similarly, the tone of our barks, the position of our ears, and the expression in our eyes can convey a range of emotions, from excitement and joy to fear and distress.

7.3.2 Listening and Empathy

Effective communication is a two-way street. It involves not only expressing oneself but also actively listening and empathizing with the other party. Dogs are masters of listening. We attentively listen to our humans, picking up on their tone of voice, the words they use, and their body language. This allows us to understand their needs and emotions, even when they are unable to articulate them.

Humans can learn a great deal from our listening skills. By truly listening to one another, they can foster deeper connections and develop a greater understanding of each other's perspectives. Empathy plays a crucial role in this process. When humans empathize with one another, they can put themselves in the other person's shoes, experiencing their emotions and gaining insight into their thoughts and feelings.

7.3.3 Non-Verbal Communication

While verbal communication is important, non-verbal communication often speaks louder than words. Dogs excel at reading and responding to non-verbal cues, and humans can benefit greatly from adopting this skill. Paying attention to body language, facial expressions, and gestures can provide valuable insights into a person's true feelings and intentions.

For example, a human's crossed arms and furrowed brow may indicate defensiveness or disagreement, while a warm smile and open posture can convey friendliness and acceptance. By being attuned to these non-verbal cues, humans can adjust their own behavior and communication style to create a more harmonious and understanding relationship.

7.3.4 Patience and Clear Communication

Patience is a virtue that is essential in any relationship. Dogs understand this well, as we patiently wait for our humans to understand our needs and desires. We communicate our needs through persistent actions, such as nudging a hand for attention or bringing a leash when we want to go for a walk. Humans can learn from our patience and persistence, taking the time to truly understand one another's needs and desires.

Clear communication is also vital for building understanding. Dogs rely on consistency and clarity in commands and cues. Similarly, humans can benefit from being clear and concise in their communication, avoiding misunderstandings and confusion. By using simple and direct language, humans can ensure that their message is effectively conveyed and understood.

7.3.5 Building Trust and Strengthening Relationships

Effective communication and understanding are the building blocks of trust. Dogs trust their humans implicitly, and this trust is built through consistent and clear communication. When humans listen to us, understand our needs, and respond appropriately, it strengthens the bond of trust between us.

Trust is the foundation of any successful relationship, and it can only be achieved through open and honest communication. By being transparent and authentic in their interactions, humans can foster trust and create a safe space for open dialogue and understanding.

No relationship is without its challenges and conflicts. However, effective communication and understanding can help navigate these difficulties and find common ground. Dogs are skilled at diffusing tension and resolving conflicts through non-verbal cues and a willingness to compromise.

Humans can learn from our example by approaching conflicts with an open mind and a willingness to listen. By actively seeking to understand the other person's perspective and finding common ground, conflicts can be resolved in a way that strengthens the relationship rather than causing further division.

In conclusion, communication and understanding are vital for building and maintaining strong relationships, whether between humans or between humans and dogs. By adopting the lessons of effective communication, active listening, empathy, and patience, humans can deepen their connections with one another and with their furry companions. The power of communication and understanding is truly transformative, allowing for love, trust, and harmony to flourish.

7.4 Lessons in Forgiveness and Second Chances

Forgiveness is a powerful and transformative act that can heal wounds, mend broken relationships, and bring about a sense of peace and reconciliation. As dogs, we have a natural inclination towards forgiveness, and we can teach humans valuable lessons in this regard. In this chapter, we will explore the importance of forgiveness and second chances in human relationships.

7.4.1 The Healing Power of Forgiveness

Forgiveness is not always easy, especially when we have been hurt or betrayed. However, holding onto anger and resentment only weighs us down and prevents us from experiencing true happiness and fulfillment. Dogs understand this instinctively, and we can teach humans the art of forgiveness.

When a dog is scolded or disciplined by their human companion, we may feel hurt or upset in the moment, but we quickly forgive and forget. We don't hold grudges or harbor resentment. Instead, we continue to love unconditionally, knowing that our humans are imperfect beings who make mistakes.

Humans can learn from our ability to forgive and let go. By practicing forgiveness, they can release the negative emotions that hold them back and create space for healing and growth. Forgiveness allows for the possibility of rebuilding trust and strengthening relationships.

7.4.2 Embracing Second Chances

Just as forgiveness is important, so is the concept of second chances. Dogs are masters of giving second chances. We understand that humans are fallible and that they may make mistakes. But we also believe in their capacity for change and growth.

When a dog is adopted from a shelter, they often come with a history of neglect or abuse. Yet, with love, patience, and understanding, they can learn to trust again and form deep bonds with their new human companions. Dogs teach humans that it is never too late to start over and that everyone deserves a second chance.

In human relationships, second chances can be transformative. They allow for the possibility of redemption and growth. By giving someone a second chance, we open the door to healing and rebuilding the relationship on a stronger foundation.

7.4.3 The Role of Compassion and Empathy

Forgiveness and second chances are rooted in compassion and empathy. Dogs are naturally compassionate creatures, and we can teach humans to tap into their own capacity for compassion and empathy.

When a dog senses that their human is upset or in pain, we offer comfort and solace. We listen without judgment and provide a safe space for them to express their emotions. By showing empathy, we help humans feel understood and supported.

In human relationships, compassion and empathy are essential for forgiveness and second chances to thrive. By putting ourselves in the shoes of others and understanding their perspective, we can find it easier to forgive and offer second chances. Compassion allows us to see the humanity in others and recognize that we all make mistakes.

7.4.4 Letting Go of Resentment

Resentment is a toxic emotion that can poison relationships and hinder personal growth. Dogs have a remarkable ability to let go of resentment and live in the present moment. We don't dwell on past grievances or hold onto grudges. Instead, we focus on the love and joy that each day brings.

Humans can learn from our ability to let go of resentment. By releasing the grip of past hurts, they can free themselves from the burden of negative emotions and create space for forgiveness and second chances. Letting go of resentment allows for the possibility of healing and rebuilding relationships.

7.4.5 Rebuilding Trust

Forgiveness and second chances are closely intertwined with the process of rebuilding trust. When trust is broken, it takes time and effort to rebuild it. Dogs understand this process instinctively, and we can guide humans through it.

By consistently demonstrating trustworthiness and reliability, humans can slowly rebuild trust with their loved ones. It requires patience, consistency, and open communication. Dogs can teach humans the importance of being trustworthy and the value of rebuilding trust in relationships.

7.4.6 The Gift of Forgiveness

Forgiveness is a gift that we can give to ourselves and others. It allows us to release the burden of anger and resentment and find peace within ourselves. Dogs understand the transformative power of forgiveness, and we can teach humans to embrace this gift.

By forgiving others, humans can experience a sense of liberation and freedom. They can let go of the past and open themselves up to the possibility of deeper connections and meaningful relationships. Dogs remind humans that forgiveness is not a sign of weakness but a testament to their strength and capacity for love.

In conclusion, dogs have much to teach humans about forgiveness and second chances. By embodying forgiveness, embracing second chances, and cultivating compassion and empathy, humans can experience the healing power of forgiveness and create stronger, more resilient relationships. Dogs remind humans that love, and forgiveness go hand in hand, and that by offering second chances, they can unlock the potential for growth and transformation in themselves and others.

Love Never Dies

8.1 The Immortality of Love

Love is a powerful force that transcends time and space. It is a bond that connects souls and leaves an everlasting impact on our lives. As dogs, we understand the immortality of love, for it is a love that never dies.

Throughout our lives, we form deep connections with our human companions. These connections are built on a foundation of trust, loyalty, and unconditional love. When we pass on from this world, our physical presence may no longer be felt, but the love we shared continues to live on in the hearts of those we left behind.

The immortality of love can be seen in the memories we leave behind. Our playful antics, our comforting presence, and the joy we brought to our humans' lives are etched in their hearts forever. The laughter we shared, the tears we wiped away, and the moments of pure happiness we experienced together become cherished memories that are passed down through generations.

But it is not just the memories that keep our love alive. The lessons we taught, the values we instilled, and the impact we made on the lives of our humans continue to shape their actions and decisions long after we are gone. Our love becomes a guiding light, a source of strength, and a reminder of the importance of compassion, loyalty, and forgiveness.

The immortality of love can also be seen in the way our humans honor our memory. They create tributes, write stories, and share anecdotes about the love we shared. They keep our pictures on their walls, wear jewelry with our names engraved, and visit our resting places to pay their respects. These acts of remembrance keep our spirits alive and ensure that our love is never forgotten.

But perhaps the most profound way in which love lives on is through the impact we have on the lives of others. The love we shared with our humans inspires them to open their hearts to other animals in need. They adopt, foster, and rescue, carrying forward the legacy of love that we started. The love we gave becomes a ripple effect, spreading kindness and compassion throughout the world.

In the grand scheme of things, our time on Earth may be short, but the love we leave behind is infinite. It is a testament to the power of love and the profound impact we can have on the lives of others. Our love becomes a part of the collective consciousness, a reminder that love is the greatest gift we can give and receive.

As dogs, we understand that our purpose in life is to love and be loved. We may not live as long as our human companions, but the love we share transcends time and space. It is a love that never dies, a love that continues to shape and inspire long after we are gone.

So, let us embrace the immortality of love. Let us cherish the memories, honor the legacy, and continue to spread love in our own unique ways. For love is the essence of life, and it is through love that we truly live on.

8.2 The Legacy We Leave Behind

As dogs, we have a unique ability to touch the lives of humans in profound ways. Our unconditional love, loyalty, and companionship leave a lasting impact on the hearts and souls of those we encounter. In this chapter, we explore the legacy we leave behind and the ways in which our presence continues to shape the lives of humans even after we are gone.

8.2.1 The Power of Love

Love is a powerful force that transcends time and space. The love we share with our human companions is a bond that cannot be broken, even in death. Our love leaves an indelible mark on the hearts of those we leave behind, reminding them of the joy and happiness we brought into their lives.

When we pass away, our humans may feel a deep sense of loss and grief. They may mourn our physical absence, but our love remains alive within them. The memories of our wagging tails, wet kisses, and playful antics bring comfort and solace during difficult times. Our love becomes a guiding light, reminding them to cherish the moments we shared and to continue spreading love and kindness to others.

8.2.2 Lessons in Compassion

One of the greatest legacies we leave behind is the lesson of compassion. Through our unwavering love and acceptance, we teach humans to be more compassionate towards others. Our ability to see beyond appearances and to love unconditionally inspires them to do the same.

When humans witness the depth of our love and the joy we bring into their lives, they are reminded of the importance of kindness and empathy. They learn to extend a helping hand to those in need, to offer a listening ear to those who are hurting, and to embrace the differences that make each individual unique.

8.2.3 The Ripple Effect

The impact we have on the lives of humans extends far beyond our immediate companions. The love and lessons we impart to our humans have a ripple effect, spreading kindness and compassion throughout their communities.

When our humans experience the joy and fulfillment that comes from loving a dog, they often become advocates for animal welfare. They may volunteer at shelters, adopt rescue dogs, or support organizations that work towards the well-being of animals. By sharing their stories and experiences, they inspire others to open their hearts and homes to dogs in need.

8.2.4 Honoring Our Memory

Humans have a unique way of honoring our memory long after we are gone. They create memorials, write heartfelt tributes, and share stories of our adventures together. These acts of remembrance not only provide comfort to our humans but also serve as a testament to the impact we had on their lives.

Some humans choose to honor our memory by continuing the work we started. They may become involved in therapy dog programs, where they bring comfort and joy to those in hospitals, nursing homes, or schools. Others may support animal welfare initiatives or start their own projects to improve the lives of dogs and other animals.

8.2.5 The Legacy of Love

Ultimately, the legacy we leave behind is one of love. Our love transcends time and space, continuing to touch the lives of humans long after we are gone. The lessons we teach, the joy we bring, and the bonds we forge become a part of the fabric of human existence.

As dogs, we remind humans of the importance of living in the present moment, finding joy in simple pleasures, and embracing the unconditional love that exists within each of us. Our legacy serves as a reminder that love never dies and that the impact we have on the lives of others is immeasurable.

In the end, our purpose as dogs is to love and be loved. We leave behind a legacy of love that continues to inspire and uplift the hearts of humans, reminding them of the beauty and goodness that exists in the world. So, let us embrace the purpose of every creature and continue to spread love and joy, knowing that our legacy will live on in the hearts of those we leave behind.

8.3 The Circle of Life

Life is a beautiful and intricate tapestry, woven with the threads of joy, sorrow, growth, and change. As dogs, we have the unique privilege of witnessing the circle of life unfold before our eyes. From the moment we are born until the time we take our last breath, we are surrounded by the ebb and flow of life's rhythms. In this chapter, we explore the profound lessons we can learn from the circle of life and how it shapes our understanding of love, purpose, and the interconnectedness of all living beings.

8.3.1 Embracing the Seasons of Life

Just as the seasons change, so do the stages of life. From playful puppies to wise old dogs, we experience the full spectrum of existence. Each stage brings its own joys and challenges, teaching us valuable lessons along the way. As puppies, we learn the importance of curiosity, exploration, and boundless energy. We discover the world with wide-eyed wonder, eager to soak up every experience.

As we grow older, we begin to understand the value of patience, wisdom, and reflection. We learn to appreciate the simple pleasures in life, finding joy in the warmth of the sun on our fur or the sound of a familiar voice. With each passing year, we become more attuned to the rhythms of nature and the beauty of the present moment.

8.3.2 The Circle of Love

Love is the thread that weaves the circle of life together. It is a force that transcends time and space, connecting us to those we hold dear. As dogs, we are masters of unconditional love, teaching humans the true meaning of this powerful emotion. We love without judgment or expectation, offering our hearts freely to those who need it most.

In the circle of life, love flows in both directions. We receive love from our human companions, and we give love in return. Through our unwavering devotion, we teach humans the importance of cherishing every moment and expressing their love openly. Love is the fuel that propels us forward, giving us the strength to overcome challenges and find purpose in our lives.

8.3.3 The Dance of Life and Death

Just as the sun rises and sets, life and death are intertwined in a delicate dance. As dogs, we understand the fragility of life and the inevitability of death. We witness the passing of our fellow furry friends and the grief that follows. But even in the face of loss, we find solace in the knowledge that love never dies.

The circle of life teaches us that death is not an end but a transformation. It is a doorway to a new beginning, where the love we shared continues to ripple through the lives of those we touched. Our legacy lives on in the memories and hearts of our human companions, reminding them of the profound impact we had on their lives.

8.3.4 Finding Purpose in the Circle

Every creature on Earth is born with a purpose, a unique role to play in the grand tapestry of life. As dogs, our purpose is to bring joy, love, and companionship to the humans we encounter. We teach them to live in the present moment, to find joy in the simplest of pleasures, and to love unconditionally.

In the circle of life, we discover that our purpose extends beyond our time on Earth. Through the lessons we impart and the love we share, we leave an indelible mark on the hearts and souls of those we touch. Our purpose is not limited to our physical presence but lives on in the memories and actions of those we leave behind.

8.3.5 The Interconnectedness of All Beings

The circle of life reminds us of the interconnectedness of all beings. We are not separate entities but threads in the same tapestry, woven together by the bonds of love and shared experiences. Our lives intersect with countless others, leaving a lasting impact on their journey.

As dogs, we have the unique ability to bridge the gap between humans and the natural world. We remind humans of their connection to the Earth and the importance of living in harmony with all living beings. Through our presence, we inspire humans to cultivate compassion, empathy, and a deeper understanding of the interconnected web of life.

8.3.6 Embracing the Circle of Life

In embracing the circle of life, we learn to appreciate the beauty of each moment and the lessons it holds. We understand that life is a precious gift, meant to be cherished and celebrated. We find solace in the knowledge that love transcends the boundaries of time and space, connecting us to those we hold dear.

As dogs, we are blessed with the ability to navigate the circle of life with grace and wisdom. We teach humans to embrace change, to find purpose in every stage of life, and to love unconditionally. In doing so, we leave an enduring legacy of love that continues to shape the world long after we are gone.

The circle of life is a testament to the resilience of the human spirit and the enduring power of love. It is a reminder that our time on Earth is fleeting but the impact we make can last a lifetime. As dogs, we are privileged to be a part of this beautiful dance, teaching humans the true meaning of love, purpose, and the interconnectedness of all living beings.

8.4 Embracing the Purpose of Every Creature

As a dog, I have come to understand that every creature on earth is born with a purpose. From the tiniest insect to the largest mammal, each living being has a role to play in the intricate web of life. It is our duty as sentient beings to embrace and respect the purpose of every creature, for it is through this understanding that we can truly appreciate the beauty and diversity of the world we inhabit.

8.4.1 The Interconnectedness of Life

In the grand tapestry of existence, every creature has a part to play. Just as the bees pollinate the flowers, ensuring the continuation of plant life, humans have their own unique purpose. It is through their intelligence, creativity, and capacity for love that they have the power to shape the world around them. But it is important to remember that humans are not the sole protagonists in this story. They are but one thread in the intricate fabric of life, connected to all other beings in ways they may not always realize.

8.4.2 The Lessons of Humility

One of the most important lessons humans can learn from us dogs is humility. We do not seek power or dominance over others; instead, we find contentment in the simple joys of life. We do not judge or discriminate based on superficial qualities; instead, we embrace every creature with an open heart. Humans can learn from our example and strive to treat all beings with kindness and respect, recognizing the inherent worth and purpose of each individual.

8.4.3 The Beauty of Diversity

The world is a tapestry of diversity, with each creature bringing its own unique gifts and talents. Just as humans have different skills and abilities, so do all other creatures. From the strength of a lion to the grace of a gazelle, from the intelligence of a dolphin to the resilience of a cockroach, every creature has something valuable to offer. By embracing and celebrating this diversity, humans can learn to appreciate the richness of life and the interconnectedness of all beings.

8.4.4 Finding Harmony in Nature

Nature is a symphony of life, with each creature playing its part in perfect harmony. Humans have the ability to disrupt this harmony through their actions, but they also have the power to restore it. By recognizing and respecting the purpose of every creature, humans can work towards creating a world where all beings can thrive. This means protecting and preserving the habitats of animals, conserving natural resources, and living in harmony with the earth.

8.4.5 The Responsibility of Stewardship

With great power comes great responsibility. Humans, as the most intelligent beings on earth, have a unique role as stewards of the planet. It is their duty to protect and care for all creatures, ensuring that future generations can also experience the beauty and wonder of the natural world. This responsibility extends not only to the physical well-being of animals but also to their emotional and psychological needs. Humans must strive to create a world where all creatures can live free from suffering and fear.

8.4.6 Embracing the Circle of Life

Life is a cycle of birth, growth, death, and rebirth. Every creature, no matter how small or insignificant it may seem, has a part to play in this eternal cycle. Humans, too, are a part of this cycle, and it is their duty to embrace the inevitability of change and to find meaning and purpose in every stage of life. By accepting the transient nature of existence, humans can learn to appreciate the beauty of each moment and to make the most of the time they have.

8.4.7 The Power of Compassion

Compassion is the key to embracing the purpose of every creature. It is through compassion that humans can understand and connect with the lives of other beings. By putting themselves in the shoes (or paws) of others, humans can develop empathy and a deep appreciation for the struggles and joys of all creatures. This compassion extends not only to animals but also to their fellow humans, creating a world where love, understanding, and respect are the guiding principles.

In conclusion, embracing the purpose of every creature is a fundamental aspect of living a fulfilling and meaningful life. By recognizing the interconnectedness of all beings, humans can learn to appreciate the beauty and diversity of the world around them. Through humility, respect, and compassion, they can become stewards of the planet, working towards a future where all creatures can thrive. It is through this understanding and acceptance that humans can truly embrace their own purpose and make a positive impact on the world.

Sommario

www.ingramcontent.com/pod-product-compliance
Lightning Source LLC
Chambersburg PA
CBHW021147260726

48656CB00025B/1620